TWAYNE'S WORLD AUTHORS SERIES

A Survey of the World's Literature

Sylvia E. Bowman, Indiana University

GENERAL EDITOR

NEW ZEALAND

Joseph Jones, University of Texas

EDITOR

R. A. K. Mason

(*TWAS* 130)

TWAYNE'S WORLD AUTHORS SERIES (TWAS)

The purpose of TWAS is to survey the major writers —novelists, dramatists, historians, poets, philosophers, and critics—of the nations of the world. Among the national literatures covered are those of Australia, Canada, China, Eastern Europe, France, Germany, Greece, India, Italy, Japan, Latin America, New Zealand, Poland, Russia, Scandinavia, Spain, and the African nations, as well as Hebrew, Yiddish, and Latin Classical literatures. This survey is complemented by Twayne's United States Authors Series and English Authors Series

The intent of each volume in these series is to present a critical-analytical study of the works of the writer; to include biographical and historical material that may be necessary for understanding, appreciation, and critical appraisal of the writer; and to present all material in clear, concise English—but not to vitiate the scholarly content of the work by doing so.

R. A. K. Mason

By CHARLES DOYLE

University of Victoria
British Columbia

Twayne Publishers, Inc.   ::   New York

Preface

In a small community special difficulties inevitably attend any attempt to write a biography of a living person. I am conscious that the chief inadequacy of the study which follows is a biographical one. Very few of Mr. Mason's private papers have been made available. Some of his friends and acquaintances have been co-operative and one or two valuable insights were gained through talking with them or corresponding with them, but circumstances generally have impelled me to confine direct biographical data largely to one chapter of this book and then almost wholly to summarize material already quite widely known in New Zealand. By far the greater part of this book, then, is critical. Because this is the first full-length study of Mason's work (or, for that matter, of the work of any New Zealand poet) I have given in chapter three an account of critical reactions to him throughout his career.

At various times I have received useful help and encouragement from Professor James Bertram, Mr. Frank Haigh, Mr. G.A. Hemus (to whom I am particularly indebted for free use of his unpublished essay on "Classical feeling" in Mason's poetry), Mr. R.B. Land, Dr. E.H. McCormick, Dr. J.C. Reid and Mr. Kendrick Smithyman. Needless to say, none of the book's shortcomings is attributable to any of them.

I am grateful to the following for permission to quote copyright material:
Mr. R.A.K. Mason and the Pegasus Press, Christchurch, for permission to quote extensively from R.A.K. Mason's *Collected Poems*; Mr. R.A.K. Mason for permission to quote from his com-

memorative talk on the late A.R.D. Fairburn; the Trustees of the Author's estate, The Society of Authors, and Messrs. Jonathan Cape Ltd. for quotations from *Collected Poems* by A.E. Housman; Mr. H.W. Donner and the Oxford University Press, London, for permission to quote from *The Works of Thomas Lovell Beddoes;* Professor Frank O. Copley and the University of Michigan, Ann Arbor, for permission to quote from *Catullus—The Complete Poetry.*

I would like to express my thanks also to the editor of Challenge Publications, the Auckland General Labourers Union, for use of the files of *Challenge;* to Mr. J.E. Traue, National Library Service, Wellington, for bibliographical material and copies of cyclostyled material which is otherwise unavailable; to Miss Kay Shedden and Mrs. Dianne Turner for typing the manuscript. I am especially grateful to my wife for her patience and help in the writing of this book.

Contents

Chronology

1905 January 10. Mason born in Auckland.
1912 Sent to live in Lichfield, Waikato.
1915 Returned to Auckland.
1916 Pupil at Panmure School.
1917 Began at Auckland Grammar School.
1919 Became friendly with A.R.D. Fairburn.
1920 Adapted "O Fons Bandusiae" into English.
1922 Left Grammar School.
1923 Issued *In the Manner of Men*.
1924 Published *The Beggar*. Began work as a Tutor at the University Coaching College. Two poems published in *The Chapbook*, London.
1925 Published *Penny Broadsheet*.
1926 Began part-time university study.
1928 First journalistic publication.
1929 Stopped university studies. Gave up Coaching College tutorship. Two of his poems published in Harold Monro's anthology, *Twentieth Century Poetry*.
1930 Farm labouring, with Fairburn, in Waikato. Fairburn went to Europe. Two of Mason's poems published in the anthology *Kowhai Gold*.
1931 Marked increase in journalistic output. Items mainly political.
1932 "On the Swag" published in England.
1933 Edited *Phoenix*.
1934 *No New Thing* published. One poem included in the English anthology, *The Modern Muse*.

1936   Caxton Press founded. *End of Day* published.
1938   *Squire Speaks* published. "To Save Democracy" published
       in *Tomorrow*. Resumed university studies.
1939   Graduated B.A. Many contributions to *The People's Voice*,
       a weekly founded mid-1939.
1941   *Help Russia or—Help Hitler!* published. *This Dark Will
       Lighten, Selected Poems* 1923-41, published.
       Recent Poems, with Curnow, Fairburn and Glover pub-
       lished.
       Edited *In Print,* which replaced the Government-banned
       People's Voice.
1943   *China* published. *The People's Voice* resumed publication,
       with Mason listed as publisher.
1944   Became General Editor of the new union newspaper,
       Challenge.
1945   *Refugee* produced by Margaret Barr (with *China*). Allen
       Curnow *A Book of New Zealand Verse* published.
1947   *Frontier Forsaken* published.
1948   Lectured in Dunedin on the idea of a national theatre.
       Resigned *Challenge* editorship. Continued to work on the
       paper and in union.
1950   "Sonnet to MacArthur's Eyes" published.
       Mason published several issues of *Congress News.*
1956   Gave up union work and *Challenge* journalism. Became
       landscape gardener.
1957   A.R.D. Fairburn died. Mason visited China.
1962   January 10, Mason left Auckland for Dunedin to take up
       the Burns Fellowship at the University of Otago.
       Collected Poems published.
       China Dances published.
1964   Married in Dunedin.
1965   Mason returned to Auckland, where he now lives.

CHAPTER ONE

General Background

S MALL, remote, new — these words aptly describe New Zealand, whose tiny, narrow land mass is set in the middle of vast oceans. Australia, her nearest neighbour of any size, is more than a thousand miles away. Colonized only in the very early years of Queen Victoria's reign, New Zealand could hardly be situated further from the land in which its first organized settlement was planned and from which its first large groups of European settlers sailed in the eighteen-forties.

Only time will change both the brevity of New Zealand's history and its geographical remoteness. Even today, and especially outside its four main centres, it is a thinly populated country. The effects of remoteness and newness are, it seems, compounded by the country's physical size. Australia, because of its very vastness and vast resources alone, is rapidly becoming a world power and thereby playing an important part in world events. This must affect its place in the world, its attitude to the world and, ultimately, the quality of its daily life. It is common today for visitors to find New Zealand a "quiet" country compared with its giant neighbour.

Early Poetic Responses

Newness, remoteness, smallness—these are attributes of his country which the New Zealand writer, at any rate the *pakeha*[1] writer, cannot avoid recognizing. Those few of our nineteenth-century poems which are not slavish imitations of English models were, all the same, necessarily conscious of our dependence:

11

But for us the morning's garland
Glistens still with evening's dew;
We—the children of a far land,
And the fathers of a new.

The division hinted at in these lines of C.C. Bowen[2] haunts us
still, a little. What lifts Bowen himself a step above other
nineteenth-century New Zealand versifiers is suggested in a
sentence of his "Moonlight in New Zealand":

On our midday path
Our bodies cast no shadows, and our minds,
To sterner purpose turned, refuse to trace
The shadowy lands of Hope and Memory.[3]

A haunted sense of loss and dislocation is characteristic of
our few sensitive poems of that age. Another poet, Edward
Tregear, lamented the "ghastly peace" which had pervaded the
uninhabited and lonely land from when it had been "a drop
of molten stone." He sighed:

All still, all silent, 'tis a songless land,
That hears no music of the nightingale.[4]

William Pember Reeves, a leading figure in New Zealand's
brief history,[5] could view the problem, the inevitable dichotomy,
more objectively. The protagonist in his poem "A Colonist in
His Garden" receives a letter from a friend advising,

Old Friend, ere darkness falls, turn back
To England, life and art.

The Colonist answers:

'No art?' Who serve an art more great
Than we, rough architects of State
With the old Earth at strife?

However, when he explains how one "architect" is proceeding
we realise that his aim is to create under the "Skies, without
music" a model of England:

> Skies, without music, mute through time,
> Now hear the skylark's rippling climb
> Challenge their loftier dome.
> And hark! A song of gardens floats,
> Rills, gushes clear—the self-same notes
> Your thrushes flute at Home.

For nearly a hundred years it is as if our poets moved and lived in their country without truly seeing it or sensing it except in those few rare moments cited. For almost all, their imaginations could not come into contact with the country because their hearts and minds were elsewhere. Many made no attempt to absorb the land in which they passed their daily lives. Their attempts to describe it derived from literary sources rather than observation. This situation did not change until the beginning of R.A.K. Mason's career in the early nineteen-twenties.

A National Identity

Particularly since the nineteen-thirties one stream of our writers, poets especially, has been much preoccupied in searching for and anatomizing New Zealand's identity as a nation. One of these, the essayist and critic M.H. Holcroft, observed (in 1940, the country's Centennial year):

> It is shattering to go abroad and discover how small a place these islands occupy in the seas that surround them and in the minds of continental peoples, especially in the regions where the human swarm is at its thickest. There are so many places where New Zealand is not even a name; even in Britain it remains a symbol of remoteness for millions of persons.[6]

Much more recently, at the University of Auckland, a series of lectures was given on "the effects of remoteness on New Zealand."[7] One is that the country occupies little or no place in the minds of those who live elsewhere. Beyond its production of wool, mutton and butter little in New Zealand's past or present offers itself to the outsider that he may form an "image" of the country. This very lack presents a problem to the writer which may be at least partly technical. If he speaks too exclusively to his own people will he have any audience to mention at all?

Our national insignificance and irrelevance is not, however, complete. In *Distance Looks Our Way*, Keith Sinclair can go as far back as Samuel Butler in the late nineteenth-century to suggest that we were not even then as remote as all that. In the same collection, we find R.M. Chapman asserting categorically that

. . . New Zealanders, despite their physical remoteness from New York, London and Paris, are part of the world-wide dialogue of European civilisation. Our most sensitive intelligences have devoted themselves to articulating authentically New Zealand attitudes, a national pattern which all have shared in creating and feeling. But we live in an age when national differences constitute no more than regional variations on international modes of living.[8]

That is another crux for the New Zealand writer. The country as a whole has become aware of a drive to discover its own national identity at a time when all English-speaking, indeed all Western, countries are becoming progressively more like one another. To insist on pushing against such a trend could lead to eccentricity and unreality. For the individual writer to dedicate himself to pursuing, above all else, the search for our national identity, this means an inevitable distortion of his view of the world. Not our isolation, but our actual and inevitable contact with Britain and America tends to make us provincial. We are a peripheral unit in the complex of Western civilisation. We must accept ourselves as provincial, but the term "provincial" is not necessarily pejorative, merely descriptive. If we try to avoid it we are trying to avoid the truth.

Ours is a dependent culture, and the thought of what happens, of how things are done, in Britain and in the United States of America, is never far from us. Many people throughout the world may never have heard of us, but we cannot overlook them. Whatever genuine New Zealand attitudes have been discovered and analysed will be of immense value to us, but they can hardly matter much to the rest of the world. As C.K.

Stead puts it, "It is the combination of remoteness and *insignificance* which New Zealand writers feel."[9]

This insignificance has not diminished with a shift in our attitude towards the outside world, Britain in particular. Although the habit has now all but disappeared, it was possible only a few years ago, in the period just after the end of the Second World War, to hear older people refer to Britain as "Home." If New Zealanders felt remote in those years, and in the century that preceded them, it was because they were a long way from "Home." If we now feel at home in our own land, hard fact will not allow us to forget *its* remoteness from almost everywhere else. The changed attitude, become common in the past decade, is discernible in the work of our most perceptive writers twenty or thirty years earlier.

Although the Maoris have populated New Zealand since European Mediaeval times, Europeans have been at home here for only four or five generations. Maoris and Europeans exist in calm juxtaposition, but Maori art, life and mythology has not penetrated to any depth into the European imagination. For the most part our poets use Maori material self-consciously when they use it at all.

Development Since the 1920's

Yet New Zealand has changed a great deal over the past two generations. R.A.K. Mason grew to maturity in an ethos very different from that of today. During the First World War the country slavishly followed Britain's lead and her troops became part of the fighting forces at Gallipoli and on the Western Front. Gallipoli was New Zealand's "blooding" in an international war, so that today it still casts a long shadow in the popular imagination, creating an insular tendency to forget that any British troops participated in that long and bloody campaign. Nor is the practical outcome stressed, but only the glory, for us, of that struggle.

At the time of the Gallipoli campaign, William Massey, "Farmer Bill," New Zealand's Prime Minister, was only one-third of the way through a term of office which persisted until

1925. He and his party governed the country throughout Mason's formative years, and Massey's political approach was based on a cliché of the day, that New Zealand was "the Empire's outlying farm."[10] National life's whole emphasis was on cosseting the farmers. So little was Massey interested in industrial problems that he was capable of suggesting to the trades unions that they raise workers' wages by having them work longer hours. Such lack of imagination was typical of the country's life.

Immediately after the First World War, however, the Labour movement began a notable rise politically, and this in spite of a widespread feeling that the movement as a whole lacked proper patriotic sentiment. At that stage also there was a credit boom (tied to economic developments in Europe) which continued for a year or two. On heavy mortgages, thousands of returned soldiers purchased small farm freeholdings. The boom did not last and it was followed, in New Zealand, by a period of uneasy economic fluctuation which persisted throughout the nineteen-twenties. This decade, and well into the nineteen-thirties, Keith Sinclair characterizes as a time of insecurity, pervasive disillusionment, lost confidence and hesitancy, of "currency cranks" and strange religious sects and political organizations.[11] Spiritual and material panaceas were sought in the oddest places. The government itself adopted peculiar remedies. When the Depression came they thought it wrong to give unemployment relief without some material return for the expenditure involved. Consequently, the workless were doled out a pittance for doing menial and sometimes meaningless jobs. Money used to pay them was raised, at least in part, by special taxation. Men from all walks of life did this work, while the country was full of beggars and undernourished children. Rioting and looting occurred in Auckland, Wellington and elsewhere. The government deemed it necessary to enrol a special constabulary, to pass repressive legislation which encroached on individual liberty and to penalize the more liberal-minded members of the community. In Sinclair's words, "New Zealand had reached its nadir." What happened in those years was to have a permanent effect on the minds of such men as Mason

and the late A.R.D. Fairburn, New Zealand's only other poet
of distinction to emerge from that generation.

Mason as Part of the Transitional Years

Although he is still living and writing, Mason's most vital
work was done in the years 1923-1941. By the time the country
was celebrating its Centenary in 1940, he had already virtually
come to the end of his career as a poet. He continued in
journalism and wrote a number of plays, but for twenty-one
years before the appearance of his *Collected Poems* in 1962[12]
he published almost no poetry.

Yet, at about 1940, when M.H. Holcroft published his first
book of essays, New Zealand, through its writers in particular,
began to see itself more clearly. Then began what Kendrick
Smithyman calls "the phase in which New Zealand writing as-
sumed its greatest importance." This is also very early in the
phase in which the chief concern of New Zealand poetry was to
explore and define what is uniquely New Zealand's. In effect,
Mason's poetry preceded all this.

By 1941, when the Caxton Press published *This Dark Will
Lighten*, a selection from all his poetry up to that time, something remarkable had happened. During the few years before
that date the first small, but extremely valuable, body of our
writing still remarkable for its toughness and integrity had
accumulated. This was the work of writers whose sense of be-
longing to New Zealand as New Zealanders would not let them
free themselves entirely from the country as Katherine Mansfield
had done in the not too distant past, though some of them
restlessly left and returned again.

By 1941 we had the short stories of Frank Sargeson, the novels
and poetry of Robin Hyde, John Mulgan's *Man Alone* (still
one of the few really impressive New Zealand novels), the art
history and criticism of E.H. McCormick, M.H. Holcroft's influential essays, and the poetry of Allen Curnow, Denis Glover
and Charles Brasch, besides that of Fairburn and of Mason
himself. Of all these Mason appears to have been the most
solitary, most intuitive and least conscious of the part he was

playing. His curtailed career has made him seem, as a poet, a transitional figure in the sense that his work bridges the period between the wars. Until Mason our poetry had no true native impulse. A genuine local coherence has come about only in the years since he ceased writing poems.

The New Zealanders' development from being a people who saw themselves as exiles from a distant Home to the present sense of being remote and insignificant but, after all, themselves, "different; but not very," has been a long and complex one. On a graph it would not show as a continuous upward curve. Sinclair's remarks about the insecurity of the twenties are enough to indicate this. It is reflected also in our poetry. Between a period in which we produced several poets of some merit and vigour, figures such as William Pember Reeves and Jessie Mackay, and the comparative richness since the beginning of Mason's career, came a hiatus. The early twentieth century was a time of "private" poetry. The versifiers of that time completely lost touch with concrete reality. If their predecessors had some real sense of "Home," they had not. They were sentimental about a "Home" they had never experienced. On the other hand, as Allen Curnow sums it up, "they were moved by their surroundings neither to the wonder of discovery nor the rooted affection of a shared tradition."[13]

This is the background against which Mason had to work. Worthy as a handful of poems by Reeves and some others are, they offer no substantial native heritage to which our poets can turn. The versifiers of the first two decades of this century represent a vapid and debilitating influence which had to be overcome. Not surprisingly, Mason's work is not always free of the faults of imprecision common in their work. One of his strengths, on the other hand, is that he habitually rises above what, in them, has been called a "lack of any vital relation to experience."

Local Criticism and the Double Standard

When considering the context of Mason's work we cannot ignore the development of local criticism. In recent years some overseas recognition has been accorded to what has been tabbed "the flourishing New Zealand school of poets," but, although some of his poems were published in English anthologies and periodicals during the nineteen-twenties and nineteen-thirties, Mason's work is almost unknown outside his own country.

This brings us to what was a vexed question in New Zealand a decade or more ago, the necessity for a "double standard" of evaluation. It used to be a formula of sorts that a writer, although insignificant in world terms, was "major" locally. In his essay on Poe, the American poet and critic James Russell Lowell observed, "before we have an American literature, we must have an American criticism." However we may regard that suggestion, we can hardly disagree with Lowell when he adds, a little later, "Perhaps there is no task more difficult than the just criticism of contemporary literature. It is even more grateful to give praise where it is needed than where it is deserved . . . Yet if praise be given as an alms, we could not drop so poisonous a one into any man's hat."[14]

Our reviewers, from an early habit of genteel praise, have progressed through this period of concern over possible "double standards" to one in which a high percentage of our criticism is obliterative in impulse. Some of our best critics are haunted still by the spectre of the "double standard," but the wisest assume that we should expect and aim for standards which would hold elsewhere. When the matter of context is accounted for we cannot always avoid the necessity for evaluating work which might otherwise seem inconsiderable. This must be characteristic of all kinds of local context. Where context is understood there appears to be no need to resort to a grey mishmash of faint praise.

In quantity, valuable New Zealand criticism is small. A quite generous proportion of it has been devoted to Mason's work, and one chapter below gives an account of this since it is both relevant in itself and useful in detailing some of the background against which the poems were written. One of his earliest critics, Allen Curnow, is one of his best and is also a considerable poet.

Mason's work will be discussed and evaluated here in relation to no "double standard." The *Times Literary Supplement* reviewer of the *Collected Poems* assessed him as a "major minor" figure. However one may regard such labels, this seems to suggest a poet of comparable stature with, say, Hardy. The comparison does not seem an unjust one.

CHAPTER TWO

Life

Early Years in Auckland

THINLY populated, for both geographical and historical reasons, New Zealand is organised demographically around "the four main centres" situated at strategic intervals on its long, narrow, sea-divided land mass. In these, the four largest cities, dwell nearly half the country's two and three-quarter million people. Around 600,000 live in Auckland, the northernmost centre, where Ronald Allison Kells Mason was born on January 10th, 1905, and where he has spent most of his life since.

One of the two main centres located in the North Island, Auckland was the national capital a century or so ago. Today it is the commercial capital, although more than four hundred miles from Wellington, the present seat of government. Similar distances separate the two South Island centres and this, in a land where major roads and railways are relatively few, has the effect of directing people's first loyalties to whatever province they happen to live in. It divides a small, remote country, sparsely populated, into even smaller self-contained units.

A marine city placed on a narrow isthmus, Auckland sixty years ago was a medium-sized town of fewer than one hundred thousand citizens. Like all New Zealand cities and towns at that time, it was notable for the ugliness of its architecture, but of this Mason remained unaware until it was forcibly brought home to him by his school-friend and fellow-poet, Rex Fairburn. It had, and has, the bustling, improvised air of a trading centre. City and province have developed throughout the period by the expansion of dairy production and the exporting of refrigerated meats. Slow and steady in the first quarter of this century, growth

21

has been quite rapid since the mid-twenties. Regrettably, that progress has been almost entirely material.

Horse transport, still widely used during Mason's early years, indicates the pace of life. Town Hall and Central Post Office were built in successive years, 1911 and 1912. At that time the streets had been lighted by electricity for only three or four years and most private houses had yet to follow suit. It was in 1912, when he was seven years old, that Mason's family sent him to live in the tiny settlement of Lichfield, in the southern Waikato, dairy-farming country. Describing a subsequent sojourn there, nearly twenty years later, he was to recollect the area as a minute and very isolated settlement. There until 1915, most of his primary school years, he was in the care of an aunt, remembered as "rigid mid-Victorian." He claims to have been familiar then already with the work of Dickens and Shakespeare, Burns and Scott. In Burns, he shares in a national enthusiasm and has long been an active member of the Burns Society. As is suggested by one of his forenames, Kells, there is a Celtic strain in his own ancestry. Despite this he was, like Fairburn, brought up "in strict Anglican and Conservative traditions"[1] and is a descendant of pioneers. In the New Zealand ethos, an Anglican upbringing need not be at odds with a nonconformist temper, so often adduced as central to Mason.

For a year or so after leaving the Waikato in 1915, he attended primary school in the old Auckland garrison suburb of Panmure. Although it was no more than three quarters of a century old, the city had for him a colorful, romantic quality:

What a tumultuous and uproarious life this city has led. Just recently, say within the lives of the oldest men living. Since the days when the troops, as I've been told, were dragged from the grog shops and the whore shops and lashed down the road to Drury to fight a war they knew to be iniquitous. One of the first things I remember was Massey's cossacks riding into town, much to my approval at the time, I was a great Massey man at that time, I've changed a little since. Then the strikers used to file into the Trades Hall at night, pile up their weapons before they lay down on their palliasses round the walls. The gun-boat lay at the wharf with the guns turned on the town. Then the great war, the exultation when the expeditionary force went off to Samoa and the first men went overseas. And the casualty lists of the men coming through. These were men— I'm just speaking for myself—often whom I had been to school with, often just a little ahead of me.[2]

He was acutely aware of the stubbornness, the dogged persistence the war engendered in many people and remembered vividly "that incredible post-war disillusion" of a period brought to artistic life for New Zealanders in the novel *Man Alone* by his younger contemporary, John Mulgan. Mason's years of secondary education at Auckland Grammar School, an institution famous in its own country for the number of its successful scholars, were begun during the war. There in 1920 (when he was fifteen) he made his version of Horace's "O Fons Bandusiae" (*CP*, p. 41) as a homework assignment for the Classics master, a piece of work which cut through in a single stroke to his own purposes.

Two further years were to pass before he left school. From the records, his ability at most school subjects was no better than average and it was widely known of him among the masters that he found difficulty in working to a prescription. A class-mate of those days has spoken of him as "A pleasant, light-hearted, likeable rebel, always scruffy and unkempt"[3] and this thumb-nail sketch is supported and enlarged upon in various issues of the school magazine. Mason himself, typically self-dramatising, offers a somewhat different picture. Speaking of the beginning of his friendship with Fairburn, so important for both of them in those early days, he said:

At the beginning of 1919 we were both shuffled into the same fifth form . . . I was a skinny . . . lonely, ill-fitting little wretch and I well remember my pride and joy when this friendly giant took me under his wing. From our first association we had seemed to sense a community of interests . . .[5]

Sharing several classes, they commonly sat together. Each was particularly poor at mathematics and in a number of subjects it was not uncommon for both to be "bringing up the rear." Examined for matriculation at the end of that year, both failed. Fairburn left to become an insurance clerk, but Mason was to remain for three more years.

Beginnings as Poet and Teacher

Leaving Grammar School at the end of 1922, he tried various jobs briefly before becoming a tutor at the University Coaching College in Auckland. He taught Latin mainly ("up to B.A. standard"), but also Civics and Economics. At the same time he continued, at Auckland University College, the study of Classical Latin authors begun at school and this was to have a profound effect on the tone and preoccupations of all his poetry. During the six years of his tutorship he wrote much of his finest work.

Early in that period he issued *In the Manner of Men*, of which he explained:

> *In the Manner of Men* was published and it wasn't. I decided to publish it in manuscript; remember this was a fair while ago and it wasn't such a bad idea as it now seems. I had three books of good blank paper bound up by a printer and wrote at least one out. The idea was to get two more orders, covering costs. I can't remember if one went out, but somewhere I may still have a copy.[6]

The following year, 1924, he published his first printed booklet, *The Beggar*, receiving his earliest overseas recognition when Harold Monro, the poet and editor who ran The Poetry Bookshop in London, used "Body of John" and "Latter-Day Geography Lesson" in *The Chapbook*,[7] a miscellany. In the same number appeared work by Padraic Colum, T.S. Eliot, John Gould Fletcher and Sacheverell Sitwell.

Concerning the edition of *The Beggar*, something of a legend has developed. Probable "original source" of it, according to Allen Curnow (*CP*, intro. p. 10) is a 1929 article by Rex Fairburn, who believed that only a handful of copies were sold, ninety per cent being left on Mason's hands:

> He must have become sick of the sight of them in the end. I remember meeting him one day, and his telling me, half in sorrow and half in relief, that he had just been down to the end of the Queen's Wharf and had disposed of a bundle of two hundred. 'Thank God I've got a few of them off my mind, anyway!'[8]

In another version of the story, the head of the Coaching College came upon him hurling copies out of the College window into the harbour below. Much more recently, a writer claims to have asked for a copy and been given one fetched from a haul "under the bed," while yet another believes he has seen bundles being used as fuel to heat an old-fashioned water-copper.

After he had established himself as a tutor Mason began his part-time studies at the University College. The dates are variously given, but the main study period was during the academic years 1926 to 1929 and, according to University Registry records, also 1938 to 1939. Graduating B.A., his major studies were in French and Latin, his other work in Economics, Political Studies and History. His late start and the part-time character of his student career make it unlikely that, as he suggested much later during the Fairburn commemorative talk, he might well have become a Classics lecturer in the University.

When *Penny Broadsheet* appeared in 1925 it was, like *The Beggar*, published by Mason himself. It is a folded card, on which are printed five poems, an advertisement for *The Beggar*, and a dedication: "To (?) the Unknown Hero who sent me £3 in appreciation of 'The Beggar' this Sheet is Dedicated as a Token of Gratitude to himself (and a Hortatory Example to Other People!)." With his own publishing of the two works, the first of the five poems—"Song of Allegiance," amply attests to Mason's sense of vocation.

During 1926, a year of national economic uncertainty in which he began his University studies, he published nothing. For the next two years only two of his poems appeared, in local newspapers (one poem, "Stoic marching song" was printed in both Christchurch and Auckland). His output for the period also includes a slight article on free verse contributed to *The Auckland Sun* and his part in an ensuing exchange of letters on the subject. In January of 1929 we find his account of A.E. Housman's poetry in *The Auckland Star*, stressing the English poet's economy of means. Throughout all this period Mason was writing the poems which were later to be gathered into his most substantial single publication, *No New Thing*. Two of these ("Miracle of Life," "The Spark's Farewell") appeared in 1929 in Harold Monro's *Twentieth Century Poetry*. Writing to him of them early in 1930, Fairburn observed, "those two things of yours are about as good as anything in the book."[9]

In these years Mason apparently spent his summer holidays in the Waikato. Either late in 1929 or sometime in 1930 he gave up his job as tutor, choosing, as he has remarked, the eve of the Depression on which to do so. For a period he went back to the country to live: "There in 1930 I proceeded to make hay both literally and metaphorically. Though times were tough, in four months of harvesting I knocked up over forty pounds . . ."[10] That summer he was joined by Fairburn, also out of work, and this probably was the period of their closest friendship.

Mason's own account of that period, just before Fairburn left for England to become engrossed in the Social Credit theories which caused their later coolness towards one another, is most moving. They had spent an evening together, drinking and talking, with their friend Clifton Firth and his wife. At about eleven o'clock they decided to walk together to Mason's place at Ellerslie:

When we got there it would be about one o'clock in the morning, we decided it was a lovely night and we hadn't finished talking and we probably wouldn't see each other again ever, perhaps for years so we'd go home and have a yarn for a little while further and so we walked up to the top of Mount Smart—it was then a sort of mountain, it's since been mostly pulled down—and we sat there and we went on talking and we talked till the moon went down over the Manukau and the sun started to come up over the Waitemata and we went home still talking and we had breakfast, then Rex went to work. I well remember that night. I think we both had a sort of feeling, 'Well, that's the end of a sort of epoch for us'[11]

Kowhai Gold, Quentin Pope's sentimental anthology of New Zealand poetry, appeared in 1930. Without Mason's knowledge or consent two of his poems ("The Beggar," "After Death") were included. A series of provincial echoes of tenth-rate English verse, the book as a whole serves to show the impoverishment and exhaustion of the context in which he had to work. He had, however, already planned *No New Thing*. Much of his best work was an accomplished fact.

Depression Years

He also claimed to be then working on "a Polynesian racial problem." Onset of the Depression helped to focus his growing interest in politics. Curnow tells us that "the literary and political awakening of those years found Mason in touch with activities at the University of Auckland."[12] Mainly journalistic, there was a marked increase in the quantity of his published work, including several pieces on conditions in Samoa and a number of contributions to *The New Zealand Worker*, one on Germany. From England in 1932 Fairburn sent him some "Lines for a Revolutionary to R.A.K. Mason" and thenceforward, for many of his friends, this revolutionary spirit seemed the keynote of Mason's personality.

Besides contributing to the University annual *Kiwi* he played a leading part in the brief, glorious life of *Phoenix* (1932-33), whose four issues, printed by Bob Lowry, mark for many a "golden dawn" of New Zealand printing. James Bertram edited the first issues of *Phoenix*, in 1932. By the time Mason became editor, the following year, he manifested, fully and forcefully, a vital consciousness of social and political concerns.

From its beginning his political journalism achieved the tone notable in a later piece such as *Help Russia or—Help Hitler!* or *Frontier Forsaken*, through short pointed sentences in short paragraphs. Public apathy, cupidity and self-interest offered him ample targets. Throughout his career a chief theme was to be New Zealand's misgovernment of her Island Territories, his concern over which was prompted partly by a lifelong sympathy for the Maori as a racial minority. He wrote against capitalist proliferation of poverty, against militarism and against anti-Semitism. Yet when we look back through all the fruits, then and later, of his political writing it is to receive an unmistakable feeling of misdirected talent. A certain old-fashioned sense of rhetoric, a certain dogmatic stance, have inevitably kept Mason's prose less fine a thing than his poetry.

Meantime his poem "On the Swag" appeared in *The New English Weekly* and in 1934 the Unicorn Press of Auckland published *No New Thing*, a gathering of twenty-five poems written between 1924 and 1929. Lowry followed up his *Phoenix* work by designing and hand-setting the new volume very pleasantly, with broad margins, clear print and heavy Roman numerals at top and bottom of each page (numbering the poems and the pages). A hand-woven, hessian-type binding-cloth was also prepared.

Its printing history is not altogether clear, but the book had no greater fortune than *The Beggar*. Printed in a very small edition of 120 copies, of which 100 signed copies were intended for public sale, it first met trouble at the binders. Much of the edition remained at the paged-up stage. "A few copies were later bound in the special cloth for private subscribers (the Auckland Public Library has one of these, unsigned); over the years, other copies have been disposed of privately, in ordinary cloth."[13] Two copies have been sighted by the present writer, bound in the special cloth and with an inserted label reading: "This book is issued in a limited signed edition only. It has been set by hand and the type distributed. One hundred and twenty copies have been printed, and of these Numbers 1-100 are for sale. The price is a half guinea. This copy is Number —." Only a few years ago some copies of the book were put on sale in an Auckland bookshop. One of these, without endpapers, is in my possession and contains a hand-written note, initialled by Ron Holloway, another Auckland printer with an exemplary concern for his craft:

Six copies of this book were spoiled in the bindery: the proper end-papers were mislaid, and the outer pages of the first and last sections were pasted down in their place; and the edges, which should have been uncut, were guillotined excessively. R.H.4/VI 1960?

Such was the fate of Mason's most important book!

Before *No New Thing* a few articles on his work appeared, such as that by Ian Donnelly in *The Auckland Sun*, which offers a fair journalistic appraisal. With his *Phoenix* editorship, however, Mason was "discovered," from one end of the country to the other, to those few people of like mind. From the day when Denis Glover founded the Caxton Press, which he established in Christchurch in 1936, Mason's work appeared under the Caxton imprint. For the remainder of his career as an active poet he had found a publishing "home," beginning with *End of Day* in the Press's first year.

Containing only five poems, this booklet marks something of a turning-point in his career, a point at which the verse becomes allied to overt political gestures. The feeling of such a poem as "Youth at the Dance" is heralded in his only recorded publication for 1935, a short story which appeared in *Tomorrow* at the end of that year. Intended as a parable, this cites bank manager and bishop as killers of youth, youthful ideas and imagination. While the actual killing is carried out by the bank manager the onlooking crowd is depicted as remaining docile, indifferent. The piece has that tractarian presence common to all Mason's prose. While it may be "aphoristic" at its best, typically it is no more than a statement of ideas carried on a narrative line for which there is no fleshing out.

After a year in which he published nothing new, he had his one-act play *Squire Speaks* printed at Caxton in 1938. Another short play script, "To save democracy," appeared in *Tomorrow* in April of that year and he found a new journalistic source for political comment in the *Worker's Weekly*, for which he wrote on Samoa, British foreign policy, agriculture, Communism, and on a public meeting concerning the plight of China.

World War Two

With the founding of the Communist weekly *The People's Voice* in 1939 a new source became available for expression of his political views. All his writing for that year, predominantly pacifist and pro-labour in intention, appeared in the "*P.V.*" and consisted mainly of several propaganda "poems" such as "International Brigade," "The Dark Will Lighten" and "Skull on Silence," none of which has been included in any of his collections.

A year of apparent silence in 1940 (no publications for the

year are listed in Mr. J.E. Traue's bibliography[14]) was followed
in 1941 by the dissemination of a pamphlet for the Aid to
Russia Committee, *Help Russia or — Help Hitler!* and the
appearance of two books of verse which mark the culmination
of Mason's active years as a poet. A new, flowing music is
evident in his work contributed to the Caxton Press *Recent
Poems,* which brings together the work of the four most interesting poets of the immediate pre-war period, Mason, Curnow,
Fairburn and Denis Glover.

Caxton's Miscellany, *Book,* quotes a perceptive anonymous
reviewer from *The Press* of Christchurch (possibly Curnow):

> Mr. Mason wrestles with enemies in his own mind. In his six
> poems the struggle seems not to have found as full an issue in poetry
> as in some earlier pieces, but they are wrought of the same tough
> metal. Possibly they mark for him the close of a period. He is re-
> exploring his old forms and influences, and will probably require
> change before long.[15]

It was, indeed, "the close of a period." Excepting the verse dance-
drama *China* (which is close enough to his propaganda work),
no new poem of Mason's reached print until his Korea-inspired
sonnet of 1950.

The number of *Book* mentioned above contains the first penetrating assessment of Mason's talent, an essay by Curnow, and
also a note that "R.A.K. Mason's Poems have been collected and
are now undergoing a final scrutiny by the author. They will
probably be ready in July or August." *This Dark Will Lighten*
is not a collection, in fact, but a selection from the full range
of his work. Its title is nearly that of the "mass recitation" published in *P.V.* less than two weeks after war's outbreak in 1939
and performed by the People's Theatre the following December.
Mason, apparently, planned to revise and extend this for inclusion in the book. This was never done, but the Caxton selection kept its title.

The New Zealand Government declared *The People's Voice*
illegal in 1941 and in September of that year its virtual replace-
ment, *In Print,* appeared for the first time. Its odd, ironical
name was chosen because already registered as that of a peri-

odical, but not then in use. According to S.W. Scott, a former editor of *The People's Voice*, while *In Print* was not legally or openly Communist it was published to carry the Communist Party line.[16] Noting his later anti-Communist bias, there is nevertheless no reason to doubt Scott on the point. Throughout the whole run of *In Print* Mason is listed as editor, printer and publisher. The paper appeared regularly until July, 1943, and thereafter in occasional single issues, its regular publication being discontinued when *The People's Voice* regained legal status in mid-July, 1943 (it had meantime appeared illegally in duplicated form). For a few months in 1943-44 Mason was listed as publisher of the revived *P.V.*

In Print probably kept him too busy during 1942 to attend to other kinds of writing and it was not until late the following year that the dance-drama *China* was produced by Margaret Barr, an English war emigrant, for the Workers' Educational Association (WEA) Theatre. Simultaneously Mason published it: " A script was needed," he wrote, "for quite a large cast, so I got it cheaply printed, running off an extra 300 copies, which were quickly disposed of."[17]

Journalistic concerns of that time were the Pacific Islands, where unemployment and poverty were rife, and various economic matters. With the founding of *Challenge*, a weekly journal, by the Auckland Builders' and General Labourers' Union in August, 1944, Mason became General Editor. He remained so for more than four years and continued to write for the paper until 1956, when he finally left the Union organisation altogether. At first related to the war effort, with a particular slant towards the Russians, but also generally with union and national politics, Pacific Island Territories problems, the history of the labour movement, unionism and New Zealand generally, *Challenge* is not an especially distinguished publication in general terms. In its kind, especially in the early years, it has an unusual liveliness and clarity, no doubt largely due to Mason's personal judgment.

Margaret Barr produced another of Mason's plays, *Refugee*, for the New Theatre Group in 1945. Never regularly published, copies of the play were circulated (some are still extant) in duplicated form. Quite successful as dramatic writing, it is simply a piece of anti-Fascist propaganda. Five of its seven scenes are a conventionalised picture illustrating the thesis that New Zealand was itself originally populated by "refugees."

Two further years elapsed before Mason, after a trip to investigate the situation for himself, had his fullest statement on the Island Territories problem printed. *Frontier Forsaken* (An Outline History of the Cook Islands) was published under the auspices of the Auckland General Labourers' Union in 1947. *Challenge* later claimed that this brought a strong reaction from the Labour Prime Minister, Mr. Peter Fraser, who wrote in protest to firms whose advertising had helped subsidize the book.

Later Years

Late in 1948 Mason received an invitation to deliver a lecture series at Otago University, where he spoke on "The Mechanization of Culture," expressing his view of mankind's progressive dehumanisation. In those years, due to uncertain health, he rarely left Auckland. His choice of subject, quite widely reported and summarised in newspapers at the time, is conspicuously at odds with "Prelude," his optimistic programme poem written particularly for *This Dark Will Lighten.*

His journalistic interest then turned also to the question of a national theatre. Absence of overseas touring companies during the war had left a gap in which was demonstrated that New Zealand itself was capable of producing dramatic performances at a good standard. The potential for a national professional theatre seemed to be there. Mason took up the question in an article for the Christchurch *Press*, having earlier in the same year, in one of his few contributions to the quarterly *Landfall*, scoffed at the aims and standards of a private enterprise attempt at creating a New Zealand company. He was adding his vote to a project already of lively interest. A *Press* leading article supported him as did a prominent member of the House of Representatives. Possibly because the Labour Government lost its power within a year, nothing came of those particular efforts.

Both Mason's leading concerns in the late 'forties, the Island Territories' problem and the hope for a national theatre, are only now in the mid-sixties beginning to receive serious treatment. A year in which he published nothing except his *Challenge*, journalism is probably explained by ill-health. Having relinquished editorial duties late in 1948 he published no new work until April, 1950, when his one-act farce "Daddy, Paddy and Marty" appeared in *The People's Voice*. Dr. Martyn Finlay, a leading Government spokesman in the national theatre campaign, had publicly analysed the reasons for the Labour defeat in 1949, and this small play satirises his apologia. Later in the year *P.V.* also published Mason's "Sonnet to MacArthur's Eyes," a bitter comment on warriors, arising from the Korean war. Reprinted many times, widely circulated, his only verse for a decade, this has become one of his best-known pieces.

As a further sign of brief revitalisation, *Congress News*, a short-run union newspaper of about that time, is noted in its third issue as ". . . published by R. Mason, Box 9, Newton, for the N.Z.T.U.C."[20] Then, although he continued working and, presumably, writing for *Challenge*, comes a gap of seven years in which he published nothing else. Late in 1956, due to poor health, he gave up professional journalism altogether. He also resigned from the assistant secretaryship of the Auckland General Labourers' Union and began work as a landscape gardener.

Within a few months, Rex Fairburn became seriously ill and knew that he was dying. He made the effort to go and see many of his old friends in various parts of the country. A quarter of a century after his return from Europe in the early thirties he and Mason resumed the friendship which had all but lapsed completely, but Fairburn died late in March, 1957. Two or three weeks later Mason commemorated their old comradeship in a long recorded talk to the Auckland University College Literary Society.

This reveals as much of Mason himself as of Fairburn. His self-protective attitudes had not changed much in thirty years. Self-portrayed in *The Beggar* as "the old vagrant," he has now become "an impoverished and infirm old working man, isolated,

at war with the world . . . a vagabond scuffling away into the
obscurity."[21] Thus he saw himself and projected himself consciously in his work, but in our reading (in the best of the
journalism, or in "Judas Iscariot" or "Footnote to John") we
encounter someone far tougher, tenacious, capable of irony or of
going beyond it. Detailed reading of Mason strongly suggests
an artist ignorant of his own real strengths, ignorant enough
to be defeated by an unrewarding environment.

Mason was one of their chief contacts when, in 1956, a group
of members of the Classical Theatre of China visited New
Zealand. Early in the following year his speech, welcoming them
to Auckland, was translated into Chinese and published in
Peking. Towards the end of 1957, at the Peking Government's
invitation, he visited China with an official party made up
largely of intellectuals who had become prominent in New
Zealand in the 'thirties. One of these, Mason's old friend James
Bertram, was struck by the way in which Mason conveyed a
strong feeling of his empathy with the ethos and people.

China Dances, published in 1962, is comprised of a reprint
of the dance-drama *China,* the 1956 speech, and another, very
brief, speech, made at a farewell dinner in Canton in November,
1957. This is "A Hundred Thousand Blessings," which is remarkably in the spirit of Chinese poetry of the same scope:

May a hundred thousand blessings fall upon your house, O China,
May they fall like the small drops that spatter the dust,
When, after long drought, the land lies warm and waiting,
May they alight on your roof-tops like the quiet doves of peace,
Gliding down through the air as softly as the autumn poplar-leaves,
And may these blessings be all around you in all your paths,
You and your children forever.[22]

In a prefatory note, Mason observes:

In Canton, I recalled that, on an occasion when too much demanded
saying for prose to express, my Celtic forebears would invoke the right
to use the poetic principle. The murmur of agreement showed that
this was a well understood custom in China also. This poem was
published, in English or in Chinese, in the Hong Kong daily newspaper for 18th November, 1957.

Since that year a few of his earlier poems have been recovered and published. In January 1962 he moved south to Dunedin to take up the Burns Fellowship for a year at Otago University. This produced a new piece, but there is little else to be found outside the Curnow-edited *Collected Poems* of the same year. Dunedin accorded Mason some measure of the recognition he deserved. Provided with a study on campus, he at first planned to write a biography of Rewi Alley, the New Zealand writer and "free verse" poet who has lived most of his adult life in China. Ill health prevented the work.

When his Fellowship concluded Mason decided to remain in Dunedin, which had been kind to him and where he benefited much from the friendship of Charles Brasch, founder-editor of *Landfall*. Intermittent illness continued to interfere with plans for writing. During this period he was quietly married and did become well enough to construct a Scots (i.e. Dunedin Scots) dialect play, *Strait is the Gate*, which was locally performed but never "written up."

Late in 1965 Mason, with his wife Dorothea, returned to Auckland, where he now lives simply on the North Shore, teaching part-time at the nearby High School. His latest publication is an introduction to *No Ordinary Sun*, a volume of poems published in 1964 by the Maori poet, Hone Tuwhare.

CHAPTER THREE

Mason's Critics

Pioneer of a Tradition

NEW ZEALANDERS "sometimes trace from the early nineteen-twenties the beginnings of a poetic tradition which they may call their own," led in so doing by Allen Curnow, who sees Mason "by any serious critical testing as his country's first wholly original, unmistakably gifted poet."[1] 1923 dates the earliest poem in the focal Caxton *Book of New Zealand Verse*. Explicitly, introducing the *Collected Poems*, Curnow nominates Mason's booklet *The Beggar* (1924) as containing the "best reasons" for establishing that period as beginning the true tradition of New Zealand poetry.

Speaking of the brief career of the magazine *Phoenix* (1932-33), Robert Chapman says:

> Besides introducing Allen Curnow, Charles Brasch and James Bertram, the four issues of *Phoenix* presented poems by J.C. Beaglehole, A.R.D. Fairburn and R.A.K. Mason, each of whom had published before. In many ways it was Mason who was the real forerunner of the group. He had published from 1924 onwards, a series of small booklets of verse which displayed a sombre personal urgency in a taut metric that owed much to Horace and Housman. Mason's was an individual voice but the effect of his tense bare verse reinforced an impulse from overseas towards a new style of poetry and a new view of language.[2]

His poetry is more consistently an unfalsified expression of *himself* than is the verse of any New Zealand writer before him. Some critics adduce other qualities (in particular, "New

Zealandness") to account for our continuing interest in, and indebtedness to, his work; but his primary value is in his evident integrity. For this reason alone he has had, for a New Zealand poet, a fair amount of critical attention. Comment on his work is in two distinct phases. A number of critics paid him more or less close attention in the early and middle 'forties, immediately following his major phase. The second main period, of a rather different general tendency, was occasioned by publication of the *Collected Poems.* Linking these are E.H. McCormick's later view of Mason's work,[3] and Curnow's *Penguin* anthology, introduction, section 8.[4] From his essay "The Poetry of R.A.K. Mason" (1941)[5] to the *Collected Poems,* Curnow undertook four extended assessments of Mason's work.

Early Mason Criticism

Curnow's *Book* essay is the earliest Mason commentary to go to any depth. Not unexpectedly, it claims Mason as a distinctly New Zealand poet. Of his predecessors, the pioneers, Curnow says, "they learnt to know birth, life, pain and death with a new immediacy" (p. 3). This freshness of response may be discerned as one of the rewards of New Zealand life, a freedom from the clutter of existence in older countries. Though perhaps taking his cue from the Americans, Peter Bland, one of a number of contemporary immigrant poets, expresses it: "Everything is new and important simply because it *is* new . . . Objects, for instance (rocks, animals, tractors, people) now exist with a clarity and life of their own they just didn't have for me in England."[6] Bland found himself in a situation not unlike that of the pioneers. He has made capital from it, but of them we have Curnow's witty, just summation, "It might be said that they lived sagas but wrote only polite verses." For those earlier generations the "translation" from Northern Europe to the Antipodes was a "shock" (a word more than one critic uses in connection with Mason). It has resulted in, "A communal repression which has persisted in the failure of their descendants to *realise* their Pacific habitation."

Observing that overt reference to the New Zealand scene and people is not especially characteristic of Mason's work, Curnow then modifies this in terms not altogether unlike M.H. Holcroft's general line of thinking at that period. Finding in the poetry an awareness of the elemental immediacy of birth, life, pain and death, "with a corresponding appreciation of the problem of evil," he concludes that "one would expect to find in Mason, therefore, some glimpse into the unconscious mind of this island community" (p. 3).

In the early nineteen-forties a number of writers, but particularly Curnow and Holcroft, were preoccupied with the ways in which a national consciousness and national spirit develop, in considering (in Holcroft's words) "whether or not New Zealand is engaged in the task of shaping a soul, not merely as the accidental result of experiment, or as the work of chance and physical change, but in the scattered manifestations (many of which may be superficially contradictory) of some deeper impulse within the nation's life."[7] Holcroft's stance towards this problem was often one of idealistic mysticism (as when he remarks, a few paragraphs earlier than the above quotation, "The soul of a nation is that indestructible work of the collective spirit which can knit a people into a unified group . . ."). Curnow was, and is, a firm believer in the nation's looking to itself, but he soon moved on from the kind of attitude suggested here. Nonetheless, that early phrase, "the unconscious mind of this island community," reveals more of Curnow than of Mason. Yet his claiming for Mason a direct consciousness of his own place and time is not altogether without point.

> I no hint of asphodel
> amaranth ambrosia moly
> paradise nor heaven holy
> after these long pangs have found . . .[8]

How much, Curnow wonders, do such lines owe "to the isolated despair of life wrenched from roots in the world's past?" Carefully, though, he distinguished between a sense that the true New Zealand poem must necessarily be about New Zealand and the instinct "which prompts the conviction that these poems

could not have been written, could not have been given their
essential character, by any other than a New Zealander"; and he
speaks of "the distinctively native-born character of Mason's
poetry."

Before Curnow's second appraisal, in the Caxton anthology
introduction, two other noteworthy estimates of Mason's work
appeared. One of these, an essay by William Plomer in *Folios
of New Writing*, was published within months of Curnow's
Book essay. The other is in *The Waiting Hills*, volume two of
Holcroft's trilogy (1943).

Contrasting with Curnow's approval of Mason's "emotional
control . . . his compactness of structure and sure weighting
of words, and his conspicuous (especially in New Zealand) lack
of dependence on epithet . . ." E.H. McCormick, acknowledging
Mason's essential seriousness and the value of his achievement,
yet suggests that his reputation in the 'twenties had depended
upon "a habit of mellifluous rumination."[9] Plomer, referring specifically to *No New Thing*, says "Mason's chief trouble in these
and later writings, is rhetoric. He is not the only living colonial
poet who, in the use of rhetoric, has dramatised himself into a
romantic attitude: the process is no doubt one of compensation
for lack of an appreciative audience."[10] Mason's poetry possesses
"the candour of free conversation and a child-like innocence of
vision." Detecting the influence of A.E. Housman and D.H.
Lawrence, Plomer sees the poems generally as "gloomy, sexy
and sardonic . . . a heavy shadow lay over them, cast, apparently,
by Protestantism."

If Plomer's judgments were made without first-hand experience of New Zealand, Holcroft on the other hand had been
occupied for more than a decade with anatomising the New
Zealand scene. Not entirely acquiescing with Curnow that our
poetic tradition began as late as the twenties, he nevertheless
agrees: "It is only during the past twelve or fifteen years that
we have had poets whose work shows continuity of attitude."[11]
He felt that Mason's poetry "Must have received at least part
of its sinew from the impact of the slump years" (p. 162).
Indicating Mason's "consistent indifference," as poet, to the local
scene, he believed this could be attributed to Mason's discovery

of his own isolation in "an unfriendly social climate." Behind
Mason's use of "the well-known backgrounds," he saw, rather
than a deep sense of the local or national, a tendency to
universalise, "he detaches from them the universal elements that
are the properties of poetry in every country, and he infuses
them with an emotional content that turns them into landscapes
of the mind."

Curnow's Caxton anthology brought together the work of
sixteen poets, from the nineteen years-old James K. Baxter to
Arnold Wall, then in his late seventies. After twenty years, a
smaller group has now emerged from the sixteen. Fairburn,
Mason, Brasch, Glover, Baxter and Curnow himself undoubtedly
represent the main strength of our poetry up to ten or twelve
years ago. Very few of the names could be dispensed with, one
or two at most, without creating a gap. A rigorous choice from
a large number of verse practitioners and poetasters, time has
proved it largely right. Mason figures prominently in it, and
Curnow has continued to speak of his work with sympathy and
insight.

Eighteen of Mason's poems are included (only Ursula Bethell
is more generously represented), and in the book's long introduction Curnow contemplates the whole range of Mason's work.
For the first time, he refers approvingly to Mason's technical
proficiency. He is not especially concerned with the poems'
language, but with "the time-life of a poem, its rhythmic character within the chosen necessity of prosody."[12] A poem's time-
reality (i.e. the way in which the poet, within the metrical con-
vention he has accepted for the particular poem, continues to
give each syllable and phrase vitality and individuality) is "an
important determinant of value" because "the time or rhythm
cliché is more debilitating than any other, and will kill a poem
surely, for all the poet's ingenuity or sincerity." The whole matter
of technique has been raised directly in relation to Mason's
work because of the conspicuous time-reality of his poems.

Curnow links Mason with another of his own lifelong preoccupations, consciousness of the dependent nature of New
Zealand life, of New Zealand's economic, political and cultural
subordination to Britain. "We are stunted emotionally because

we have not dealt direct with life, but through intermediaries. . . . Mason, if at the cost of centring tragedy too much
upon himself, has tried to deal direct with life" (p. 33). Diverse
opinions as to Mason's freedom from rhetoric or weakness for
it, his "lack of dependence on the New Zealand scene" as opposed
to "the distinctively native-born character" of his poetry, are
matched in references to his political consciousness. "He professes Communism, but that has barely touched his verse in any
direct or dogmatic way," Curnow tells us,[13] while Alan Mulgan
(writing at roughly the same time) declares, "It is the tragedy
of the economic system rather than of human nature that moves
him."[14] Contemporaneously, Holcroft referred to "the intellectual
rash of Marxism, plainly discernible in much of our contemporary writing."[15] And J.C. Reid could say of Mason, "His retreat
into Marxism is evident fairly early."[16]

Reid's brief account is a sifting, a summing-up, of comment
on Mason's work up to the mid-'forties. It marks the end of the
first phase. To Reid, Mason seems "a naturally sensitive personality who has reacted defiantly against the demands of a
society hostile to his type of poetic utterance" (p. 33). Yet he
concedes that Mason is "genuinely a New Zealand poet in that
the spirit of his poetry, a spirit of disillusion, of frustration, of a
sense of grievance, of emptiness, and a search for a stable basis
of value is the dominant spirit of the New Zealand secular
intellectual" (p. 33). Adding to these Mason's "pessimistic
agnosticism," his "agony of spirit concerning sex" and his "morbid joy in brooding on death and decay," Reid judges that the
poems "have a stark spare quality well suited to express his
morose temper." Mason's apparent inability "to escape from religious symbols or a religious way of thinking" and his repeated
attempts "to shake off the effects of a harsh and tyrannical religious environment in early life" are seen as formatively important. Observing that Mason matured very early as a writer, Reid
adds that "there is little development evident in his later work."

At the time when these judgments were made Mason appeared
to have ceased publishing poems. Thereafter, little critical notice
was given to him for nearly a decade. No new poems reached
print until his Korean war sonnet of 1950. A further five years

then elapsed before there was brief mention of him in James K. Baxter's *The Fire and the Anvil*,[17] in which "On the Swag" is cited and quoted as an important instance of the "Man Alone" theme in New Zealand writing.

Later Criticism

Reappraisal of Mason's career in the last five or six years has been stimulated by two events—publication in 1960 of *The Penguin Book of New Zealand Verse* and, two years later, the *Collected Poems*. Immediately prior to the anthology's appearance, E.H. McCormick expressed his matured opinions of Mason's work in his *New Zealand Literature: a Survey*.[18] For McCormick now, that work has "the cold austerity of a cell." Succinctly we are told, "At the age of eighteen Mason was an accomplished poet; before he was twenty he had published some of his best verse" (pp. 114-115) and thereafter, with McCormick's customary combination of elegance and economy, follows a summary account of the poet's career and accomplishments leading to conclusions not unlike some noticed earlier— the stripped language, sombre intensity of feeling, solitariness, death-preoccupation, and the melancholy summation that, "Mason was the supreme poetic casualty in the political strife of the 'thirties" (p. 117). For a long period this has been the standard explanation for the premature curtailment of Mason's poetic career.

For one reason or another the Penguin anthology was delayed for several years. Once it was published it had neither the importance nor the relevance of the Caxton book some fifteen years earlier. This was partly because Curnow's initial task had been so thoroughly accomplished. Polished, meticulous, extensively introduced, with an expert apparatus, its chief interest centres on certain shifts in the editor's attitudes. By 1960 he had long ceased to share in, or even sympathise with, Holcroft's mystical nationalism. Himself attacked for the better part of a decade for his supposed narrow chauvinism, he made little or no attempt to rebut the charges of younger poets. Clearly now those charges were based partly on a misapprehension of some of his statements concerning *place,* but just as clearly his commentary and choice of poems for the Penguin demonstrate his determined nationalism. He selects a single poem by Katherine Mansfield on the ground that "it allows us to date as early as 1910 the emergence of New Zealand as a characterising emotional force in the work of a native poet" (p. 41). Of Mason, he mentions Housman's influence and suggests connections with elements of Beddoes and Tennyson. In a curious tone he says, "Mason's is a true personal utterance, and that of a New Zealander of the third generation. . . .". Mason's syntactical energy is such that he "must be compared with his peers, and they are . . . not very many in this century." Much is made of Mason's claim (in *No New Thing*) that he had once intended to compose "a vast medley of prose and poetry . . . expressing the whole history of New Zealand." Something like half the selection of his work (once again eighteen poems) has been chosen partly because it is possibly related to such an intention. The burden of this new examination of Mason's work is an intensified drive to see it, clearly and categorically, as primarily motivated by nationality. This thesis is maintained despite the poet's own reservations (which are not mentioned). This whole important question is examined in detail below.

Some of Curnow's mature critical positions are akin to those of Wallace Stevens. Introducing Mason's *Collected Poems* he uses a Stevens criterion to distinguish Mason's work, in stature, from that of such predecessors as Blanche Baughan, who had achieved an occasional attractive or sympathetic poem. In Mason's personal utterance he now discerns "the presence of the determining personality" and believes this to be Mason's chief significance for us. He refers to Fairburn's very early judgment that Mason's pessimism is an attitude adopted "homeopathically as a drug in order to escape from reality."[19] No, he says, these poems' virtue is their quickening of the sense of reality. Mason's almost Jacobean awareness of the darkness of human existence, his painful apprehension of man's mortality, are seen as characteristic of the "*persona,* or dramatic mask of the poet-speaker" (p. 11) and "paradoxically there is almost everywhere joy in the sheer vitality and momentum of the verse—

Gaiety transfiguring all that dread" (pp. 11-12).

In the first book-length study of New Zealand poetry, the post-war poet Kendrick Smithyman assents to Curnow's dictum that Mason's was "a condition of shocked faith." As Smithyman sees it, "Problems of faith and believing are the initial problems of Mason."[20] "Yet," he asks, "does Mason actually confront his problems?" The poems rarely attain to the condition which is their implicit end. Smithyman doubts whether the reader "receives a right emotional impact" from them and blames this upon Mason's "unguarded romanticism." Approaching the task of making a poem, Mason's weakness is to undervalue rational cohesion. Of Mason and Fairburn together, Smithyman observes, "They are emotionally lucid but only in a minor fashion are they strictly logical" (p. 66). Limited abilities partly explain this, but the central cause is a view of poetry dominated by ideas of spontaneity and "inspiration."

Substantial assessments of the *Collected Poems* were made by Roger Savage in *Landfall*[21] and C.K. Stead in *Comment*.[22] Stead also had occasion to refer to Mason in a thoughtful, if somewhat narrowly-based, consideration of New Zealand writing in *Distance Looks Our Way*.[23]

Savage's approach is iconoclastic. He discovers in Mason a writer far too self-preoccupied, "an honest, earnest doubter who thinks big, has seen Life and suffered" (p. 286). Of the masks, first posited by Curnow, he says, "Mr. Mason uses his masks as metaphors for Mason." At once violent and antithetical, or dualistic, the poetry "Celebrates a bout of tussles between opposed values." Outback versus suburbia, individualist non-conformity versus established religion, pessimistic introspection versus "cheerful superficial sensuality," a sense of the continuity of the life process versus a strong drive to stop it; ". . . Mason inhabits a purgatorial wilderness where easy euphoria and conformity are rejected in the name of the rough integrity of beggar and martyr" (p. 287). To Savage the poems read like "so many versified notes for an autobiography," the passions seem immature, inadequately expressed and communicated; Mason is frequently defeated attempting forms and arguments too complex for his capabilities.

Over all is cast "the shadow of an earnest, callow adolescent with an aching soul and an inadequate technique which are part and parcel of each other" (p. 288). Emotional glibness, technical insufficiency, tendency to cliché, indulgence in self-pity—these govern the work's quality. Cause of the foreshortened career is simply expressed: "When Marxism intervened, it seems the poet retired" (p. 289). On the evidence of *No New Thing*, Mason had just achieved a degree of mastery over his craft, but the Mac-Arthur sonnet is "as insecure technically as anything in the book." Ultimately there is "the image of a poet who has something pressing to say but is beaten to the post by the dialect in which he has chosen to say it" (p. 288). Untypical of the whole corpus are "the few fine successes."

Stead's *Comment* evaluation of Mason supports Curnow's general view in several respects. In the *Distance Looks Our Way* essay he accepts the Curnovian assertion of an essential "New Zealandness" implicit in the poems. Mason has technical strength, manifest in a syntax "strong, gaunt, spare, and almost clumsily swift,"[24] but this is not achieved by deliberation. Mason's poetic gifts were innate, his best pieces "spontaneous expressions of feelings not always perfectly understood by the mind as it brought them forth" (p. 34), the achievement "a natural, urgent lyricism unlike anything else in our poetry." Arguing cogently that young poets usually are dominated either by their "idea" (and hence their writing is technically inadequate) or by concern for form (so that their verse lacks rhythmical and emotional fluidity), Stead suggests that should a young poet consciously and deliberately achieve a syntax as compressed as Mason's he would very likely maintain it, as Mason did not. He therefore seems "a poet without a craft, a poetic medium rather than a maker of poems, a man who has been the victim of poetic occasions and a poet who is victim of the failure of those occasions" (p. 35).

Instinct and conscious thought in Mason are at variance. When the tension between them is held in some kind of balance a "meaningful ambiguity" is generated. Such an occurrence is due largely to a combination of naivety and humility, for the "philosophical" preoccupations of Mason's poetry "are those of the in-

telligent child or adolescent" (p. 35). No disparagement, this conclusion is intended to explain not only a certain simplicity, but a
freshness and immediacy, a sense of wonder, of bewilderment at
the unfamiliar, also traits of Mason's work, and lost by most of
us because of a "necessary pragmatism imposed by life itself."
Basic response in the early poems is primitivist.

These observations lead Stead to a conclusion somewhat different from those of fellow critics. While *No New Thing* admit-
tedly contains some of Mason's best poems, these are gained at a
price. The book as a whole "gives evidence of an increased self-
awareness in which the qualities distinguishing the earlier work
could not be maintained." Some poems are even self-imitative, "a
literary self-consciousness has entered" (p. 37). Earlier critics saw
in Mason a pessimist, but it would be truer to say, on the evidence of the early poems, that his is an affirmative attitude.
Dramatic in character, the best poems of *No New Thing* fit a
new concern "with the particularities of human action and human
suffering, here and now" (p. 37). Varied in mood and stance, they
lack discursiveness and are "muscular, direct and efficient."

Stead's explanation for Mason's premature coming to silence
derives from his conclusions about the poetry generally. We are
confronted with "the failure of a gift for which the will could
provide no substitute" (p. 38). The poems are valued not for
revelations on the nature of human experience, "but simply for
the feeling they impart of life itself going stalwartly and pain-
fully on" (p. 39).

This chapter has served to fill out, from another and more
specialised angle, a background for Mason's work. Much critical
comment on Mason is not generally available and, in summaris-
ing it, I hope no critic has suffered the injustice of radical mis-
interpretation. That apart, a number of problems encountered in
dealing with Mason's work have now been noted. His active
career as a poet has occupied only a small part of his life. There
is no ultimate agreement as to why this is so. Nor is there a
consensus on the degree of his technical accomplishment, or the
extent to which it developed. There is substantial, though not
entire, agreement as to his cast of mind.

These facts direct my method in ensuing chapters. No long and
complex literary development is here to trace and to analyse.

True, there is the political journalism and the dramatic work and these will not go without comment, but neither has the poetry's central relevance, though both deserve respect.

Mason is a poet of stature, if only for a relatively small number of poems. What follows is not a serial discussion of his writing career, but an examination of the poetry from various viewpoints. Each facet may reveal something of the man, which is beyond the powers of a sketchy biography derived from limited sources.

CHAPTER FOUR

In the Roman Fashion

"In the Manner of Men"

MASON's first "published collection," *In the Manner of Men*, consists of four poems,—an introductory "Lullaby" fashioned in tercets and three "Sonnets of the Ocean's Base," a sequence. Of the original "edition" of two hand-sewn manuscript copies neither is now available, although one may be among the author's papers. The second sonnet has not really been accessible until publication of *Collected Poems*. Of all four poems, only the last has been widely circulated.

Already, in "Lullaby," Mason is preoccupied with inescapable death, the implication of which will be his poetry's main theme. Certain features of the poem, such as references to "black phantoms" (st.7) and festering "like a madman's brain," seem at first reading merely stock romantic, but are enriched and deepened when related to classical burial rites and the classical concept of death.[1] Mason's way of handling the poem appears to depend on his awareness of these.

Stress is placed repeatedly, in classical literature, on the importance of correct funeral procedure in helping the dead through Hades. As in Sophocles' *Antigone*, it can provide the crux of a Greek tragedy. Ezra Pound bases a vivid moment of Canto I (adapted from *The Odyssey*, "The Book of the Dead") on this knowledge:

> . . . first Elpenor came, our friend Elpenor,
> Unburied, cast on the wide earth,
> Limbo that we left in the house of Circe,

Unwept, unwrapped in sepulchre, since toils urged other
Pitiful spirit. And I cried in hurried speech:
'Elpenor, how art thou come to this dark coast?'

It may be used as a climax, the fate of *hubris*, as in Euripides'
Electra. Electra reviles the corpse of Aegisthus with a ferocity
not unlike that of Mason's ironically titled "Lullaby." She asks
(ll.904f.): "With which of thine iniquities shall I begin my re-
cital?" The choric response conveys that Aegisthus's crime and
Electra's revenge are "terribly alike." The capitalist is a victim in
Mason's poem, but the background is recollection of his former
tyranny—he is also the oppressor.

Taking the idea of need for proper burial Mason has it, by
reversal, suggest that in death the "enemy" will find no peace:

> I have taken pick and spade
>   digged you out whence you were laid
>   midst the moan your money made
>
> Digged you out whence you were shrined
>   I whom thing with scarce a mind
>   all long lifetime you did grind
>
> Down to filthed machine-like toil . . .

At the end of stanza five, through two stanzas, the rich man's
burial-spot is evoked in terms appropriate to the classical Underworld:

> this spot hell-black
>
> Where thin vines untouched by scythe
>   leanly thrusting lank and lithe
>   like foul snakes around you writhe
>
> Where the stunted dark trees brood
>   like black phantoms . . .

Repeated use of "like" suggests an analogy somewhere in the
background. The "thin vines . . . (which) . . . like foul snakes

around you writhe" may remind us of Vergil's image of "*Discordia demens vipercum crinem vities innex cruentis*" ("Insane strife with a bloody ribbon binding her snaky hair")—*Aeneid*, VI, 280-281. Emblems of the rich man's crimes against humanity may correspond with personifications encountered at the entrance to Vergil's Hades,—Grief, Hunger, War, etc. The stunted trees and "foulness spewed" (st.7) are typical of Cocytus's deep pools and the Stygian marsh (*Aeneid*, VI, 323).[2]

The "here," "where," "where," development in the structural succession of stanzas 5-7 is Latinate. A phrase such as "till the very sun is slain" (st.9) carries a whole weight of classical suggestion, "linking as it does with ancient sun-sacrifice mythology (Rhodian, Spartan and Egyptian)."[3] Another interesting point is the peculiar use of dated vocabulary, "didst," "midst," "digged," "methinks." Mason's contemporary D'Arcy Cresswell habitually wrote lines such as

> A spirit to thine arbour draweth near

and

> Ye barren hearts and bitter, steep'd in brine

(taken at random from his sonnet sequence "Lyttelton Harbour"). Of Cresswell's diction, and these are typical examples, McCormick has observed, "the archaisms are an insuperable obstruction" to appreciation of the poetry.[4] This has not proved so, the manner being widely accepted as a mark of Cresswell's individuality. No objection has ever been raised to similar oddities in Mason's language. Nor, on the other hand, has it been suggested that such diction usually (as in "Lullaby") serves as an ironic purpose, here as a rhetorical flourish in contrast with "situation." A sense of the grandiose is set in tension against the capitalist's abysmal fate and the speaker's shocking vengefulness.

It seems odd that the three "Sonnets of the Ocean's Base" should ever have been printed other than as a group. Curiously, each poem in this collection is concerned with burial. Of the sonnets, this must be qualified. Drowned (and, in that sense,

buried in the sea) the poem's protagonist certainly is; but, in
Sonnet I sestet, he speaks of "my drowned yet sensible flesh."
These are poems of resurrection, re-birth. Here connection with
the descent to Hades is obvious. The poems have something of
the atmosphere of Jungian accounts of dreams; dream is the
initial setting,—"I dreamt that as I voyaged the ship sank." As
noted, in Homer's "The Book of the Dead" entrance to the Underworld is via "the ocean's base."

To digress for a moment, Sonnet I corresponds illuminatingly
with *Richard III*, act I, scene iv, where Clarence, just before he
is murdered, recounts a fearful dream to the dungeon keeper.
Mason's sonnet, "Omnia Vincit Oceanus," opens:

> I dreamt that as I voyaged the ship sank
>   helpless in strife with water I was whirled
>   down to a tremulous light-untroubled world
>   of strange dim shapes . . .

Dead comrades' "grinning mockeries," "dim seen" beneath "dead
sails wave-furled," are contrasted with the octet's close:

>   I saw the pearled
> proud vaulted halls where once old princes drank.

Clarence says:

> O Lord, me thought what paine it was to drowne
> What dreadfull noise of water in mine eares,
> What sights of ugly death within mine eyes,
> Me thoughts I saw a thousand fearfull wrackes:
> A thousand men that Fishes gnaw'd upon:
> Wedges of Gold, great Anchors, heapes of Pearle,
> Inestimable Stones, unvalewed Jewels,
> All scattered in the bottome of the Sea,
> Some lay in dead-men's Sculles, and in the holes
> Where eyes did once inhabit, there were crept
> (As 'twere in scorn of eyes) reflecting Gemmes,
> That woo'd the slimy bottome of the deepe,
> And mock'd the dead bones that lay scattered by.[5]

Drowned in a dark sea, the sea of chaos, Mason's protagonist comes upon "the ruined palaces of dead kings," themselves returned to chaos, whose playthings they are. "Ancient argosies" (once, presumably, filled with riches, now stripped and barren in the clutch of death) are held forth in the sea's mesh. Protagonist's own body ("my drowned yet sensible flesh"), as though dead, is "mouthed by clammy cold and hideous things" ("that Fishes gnawed upon"—*Richard III*). The locus of death, and death itself, is "that great unrelenting mesh."

Sonnet II describes the argosies' contents, their buried treasure of jewels, gold and silver. Protagonist's movement lacks purpose and direction ("I strayed where sunk fleets slept . . ."). Among bars of beaten gold and the "jacinth silver" are "swords and shields and scimitars," which tell variously of spent power, the temporality of all pomp and circumstance, of war and, finally, of man's own virility. That the sunk fleets "slept" merely presents us with a problem, but this is largely resolved by the sestet's heavy emphasis on death.

Swords and shields are likened in their coldness to:

> . . . adoration paid by a bent old
> eremite bodily prone beneath the stars.

Stock, pseudo-romantic "eremite" excepted, the poem's vocabulary is 'ninetyish. Here the figure is adequate enough to reinforce a statement rejecting an escapist way of life, to worship which would mean being out of touch with present realities, and with other human beings. This is the first abandoned, rejected and solitary figure in Mason's poetry. Too much should not be read into a stock response in one of his less successful early pieces, but behind the cliché one senses a putting away of all implied by such a figure, all that isolates us from other men. In the sestet:

> I moving among profuse-strewn splendour there
> like a rich poet's purse-proud dreams outspread
> came suddenly by black caves all bleak and bare
> of all but skeletons of sneering dead:
> then seeing shocked what bed such wonders share
> far from that cold cursed mortuary fled,

the opening "I moving" both conveys the effect of protagonist's being, in some sense, still alive and being carried along involuntarily by the sea. Near the riches, the the black caves of their obscurity, lie the "sneering dead." The word "sneering" is a tonal crux, though a weak one. A subjective response is projected outwards from fear of his joining the dead permanently in this submarine burial place. The "sneer" images his terror and causes him to flee, which suddenly he achieves the will to do. From its second line's Shakespearean pastiche, the sestet gathers strength to mount to the shock of the close, with the heavy phrase "cold cursed" holding mid-line while the explosive "f" sound echoes from beginning to end, "far from . . . fled" (the "l" sound of "fled" reinforcing the effect and taking up a link-echo from "cold").

A certain vigour typical of later work is lacking in the first two sonnets. "Poetic" language of a type later used to some ironical effect ("old ocean," "the very lees," etc.) here clutters and weakens the lines; but at the close the second sonnet gains a sudden access of strength. This is carried forward into the third, concluding, piece, "Out from Sea-bondage"—a poem of re-birth or, somewhat differently looked at, escape from the womb. The sequence as a whole is affirmative, optimistic. From the grim enmeshment of Sonnet I we advance through the flight in terror at the end of II, to:

> My body bedded in sea-midmost wave
>   with strong slow motion to calm caverns swept
>   where blew no wind but ever all things slept
>   where even the blustering surge forgot to rave.

This opening, apart from the ominous reiterate "slept," suggests a lulling, rhythmical peace. In the second quatrain protagonist is "trapped," "helpless," "given up to forms that crept/about the silent sand that sharp upleapt."[6] We realize that the opening speaks of stagnation, the whole poem is a description of the "long dark and man-dreadful days" before the birth, when:

> I moved monotonously with each altering swell
>   my rigid body drifting in small space
>   about the cold-ridged ocean-moulded shell.

An Intuitive Poetry

While they have strong points, these cannot be included among Mason's better poems. Looked at in some detail because they are his first "published" work, they have another special interest as examples of his method. A curious amalgam of strength and weakness, introduction and sequence are also a contrast. While "Lullaby" is a poem of conscious thought, the sequence has a Jungian dream quality. It is made of an intuitive poetry.

Until his latest poems, this is the only point in Mason's work where the sea is central. At least as far back as the Greek cosmologies the sea is symbol of formlessness, chaos, undifferentiated flux. Writing on "The Romanic iconography of the sea," W.H. Auden notes that the author of the Book of Revelation signifies attainment of heaven, transcendence of time, with the culminating phrase, *"there was no more sea."*[7] Thus the ship is customarily a symbol for society or the state. Illustrating with a quotation from Horace's *Odes*, Auden says, "The ship, then, is only used as a metaphor for society in danger from within or without. When society is normal the image is the City or the Garden" (p. 19). Mason uses the ship figure intuitively in his sequence, but it conveys vividly a sense of isolation in society (perhaps in a lost society), of his solitariness within it and betrayal or near-betrayal by it. Such a usage of the sea is of a piece with his romanticism. If, as Auden says, the "sea is where the decisive events, the moments of eternal choice, of temptation, fall and redemption occur" (p. 23), then these poems stand appropriately at the outset of Mason's career.

Lectures VI—VIII of William James's *The Varieties of Religious Experience* throw light on Sonnet III and on the general nature of Mason's poetry. Illustrating from Homer, Theognis and *Oedipus at Colonnus*, James says of the classical Greek sensibility, "The jealousy of the gods, the nemesis that follows too much happiness, the all-encompassing death, fate's dark opacity, the ultimate and unintelligible cruelty, were the fixed background of their imagination."[8] In Lecture VIII he distinguishes between the "once-born" and the "twice-born": "There are two lives, the natural and the spiritual, and we must lose the one before we can participate in the other." Citing Tolstoi and others, he shows the stages through which this second "birth" progresses. Before becoming "twice-born," attaining genuine spiritual life, the individual must pass through a "dark night of the soul." Tolstoi defines this experience as "an aspiration of my whole being to get out of life."

J.C. Reid took note of the sombre effects of Mason's puritanical upbringing, while Curnow described his condition as one of "shocked faith" and Stead rejected, or partially so, the common conclusion that Mason is a simple pessimist. We know of no experience, particularly recognised by Mason himself, which might be interpreted as a "dry" period of the soul, nor is the question of his "faith" so easily decided, but the sequence here, its darkness and conclusion, remarkably resembles accounts, such as Tolstoi's, of being "born again."

Classical Influences

On the sea's perils Auden quotes from two separate sources in Horace's *Odes*, Book I. *Odes* I, iii, includes the notion that the "estranging sea" was separated from land by the gods and thus to sail upon it is impious; but:

> What death does he fear who once with steady gaze
> Has seen the monster of the ocean glowering . . . ?[9]

Several other Book I *Odes* are concerned with ships carrying friends across the danger of the great waters. They express acute consciousness of the sea, its mysteries and perils. In spite of living most of his life in an isthmus city, never long out of sight of the sea, Mason's sea-consciousness owes as much to Homer, Horace and Shakespeare as to his immediate environment.

From Auckland University College prescriptions[10] we can determine that he studied Vergil (*Aeneid* VI and possibly VII-IX, XII), Livy 24, Horace's *Odes* I-IV, Tacitus' *Annals* IV and Terence's *Phormio*. Very likely he read Cicero's *De Natura Deorum* I and Horace's *Epistles* II and *Ars Poetica*. Following

1926-29 prescriptions, we know that, in reading for Greek History, Art and Literature, he had opportunity to study a considerable range of Homer, Thucydides, Aeschylus and Sophocles. By reputation, he was also a keen reader of Suetonius.

This training focused his preoccupations and greatly influenced him as a poet. This is manifest in the movement of his verse, choice of language, the very tone of many poems. Some of his own chief attitudes are Roman in temper and his cast of mind often resembles that evoked in James's words on the Greeks. When Lionel Trilling observes of Tacitus, "He is always conscious of his own despair; it is nearly a fault in him; the attitude sometimes verges on attitudinizing,"[11] that, too, is like Mason. Many of his poems "are so deeply impregnated with Roman feeling that they give the impression of a Roman thinking aloud, pondering vital questions of death, immortality and racial destiny" (Hemus). True of Mason's work as a whole, this seems particularly so of *The Beggar*.

Catullus

Responses to Catullus are frequent, though the connection Hemus traces in Mason's "In Perpetuum Vale" is rather tenuous. Catullus's deeply felt perpetual loss of his brother is true tragedy. Mason's theme is his own imagined death, and the poem well exemplifies one of his major themes, but it expresses an acute tragic sense rather than focusing on a specific tragedy.

Catullus's influence may be traced in several other poems. Two can be related to his "Lugete O Veneres," which reads, in Frank O. Copley's version:

weep, Venus; Cupid, weep
weep everyone who loves nice things
the little bird is dead, her bird,
the little bird, the darling, hers
she loved it more than anything else in the world
it was a sweet little thing
why it knew her—they were maid and mother, like.
it used to stay on her lap, never tried to get away
it hopped around (there it goes! no, it's going over this way!)

she was its mistress, it sang for her
and not ever for anybody else.
now it's going along the dark, scary road
down there
and nobody comes back from there, they say.
well, damn you anyway, damned night of hell
anything that's pretty you just have to gulp it down,
don't you?
such a pretty little bird
just had to grab it, didn't you?
it's just too damned bad.
O birdie, birdie, birdie, see what you've done
to her
she's crying, they're all swollen and red
her lovely eyes.[12]

First, Mason's "After Death":

> And there will be just as rich fruits to cull
>   and jewels to see
>   nor shall the moon nor the sun be any more dull
>   and there will be flowers as fine to pull
>   and the rain will be as beautiful
>   but not for me
>
> And there shall be no splendour gone from the vine
>   nor from the tree
>   and still in the heavens shall glow Jah's radiant sign
>   and the dancing sun on horses' sleek hides shall
>   seem no less fine
>   still shall the car sweep along with as lovely a line
>   but not for me
>
> And men shall cut no less curious things upon brass
>   still sweep the sea
>   nor no little lustrous shadow upon the sand's mass
>   cast by the little ripple above shall cease to pass
>   and radiance still shall enhalo shadows on moonlit grass
>   But not for me.

The differences are obvious enough. Apart from the fact that

Lesbia's euphemistic "sparrow" is her virtue, Catullus is being
ironical. The dead creature counts only for its effect on the
living. The sense of loss is reversed in Mason's poem. Strong
awareness of the total negation of sensual delight, total oblitera-
tion of the sensing creature, these make the poem.

Tonal resemblance to Catullus's lament for his dead brother
may be discovered also in Mason's "After Death." Having no
specific occasion and faintly tinged with self-pity, it lacks the
Latin poem's tragic stature, but both poems evoke with immediacy the sense of death's finality.

One of Mason's own poems is titled "Lugete O Veneres." There,
his loss of his girl-friend is parallel to Lesbia's loss of her
sparrow. Lesbia in the one case, the poet in the other, grieve.
The poignancy of that grief is deepened by the unheroic scale
of the lost objects, as though to say, "look how small is everything in the face of time, mutability and death." Yet, if Lesbia's
sparrow *is* her virtue, Mason is using the title for yet deeper
ironies. The girl in *his* poem has got away with her sparrow,
so the poet has to face a future of inevitable death and a
present of sensual deprivation. His only recourse is to "laugh
at the farce." Catullian tenderness has given way to harshness,
but it is a defensive harshness, a drive to cling to the known
present as opposed to the "dogs with unknown faces," the re-
minders that all things pass away.

Attention has been focused on what is an apparently haphazard mixture of direct, even vulgar, colloquialism with literari-
ness in Mason's poem, "vivid reality" seeping away into "literary
unreality" (C.K. Stead). Hemus brings up this point to suggest
that both Mason and Catullus aim for mock-heroic effects. This
certainly seems true of the Mason, but the mock-heroic is not
used in a detached or genuinely satirical spirit. Its powerful
effect is diminished by what is after all no more than petulant
self-pity.

Another Mason title, "Nox Perpetua Dormienda," derives from
Catullus's poem V, "Vivamus mea lesbia atque amemus," wherein
the poet begs Lesbia to allow them to live and love:

what do we care what those old

purveyors of joylessness say?
(they can go to hell, all of them)
the Sun dies every night
in the morning he's there again
you and I, now,
when our briefly tiny light flickers out,
it's night for us, one single
everlasting
Night.[13]

It is true that Mason's poem is less rapturous than Catullus's and that he emphasizes death rather than love in the opposition; true also that he slows down the poem's metre, making it more solemn. It still has a momentum which carries all forward to the final, life-affirming question:

What will it help us then girl not to have loved,
    chill and exposed to the rain or cramped and deep-sodded
    wet to the bone of a truth and mute and unmoved
    then whom will it help that we loved not when we
        were bodied?

Horace

Horace is the other most evident classical influence on Mason's work. Mason's widely recognized strain of pessimism is frequently counterpointed against a strong sense of the physical pleasures. Often his poems simultaneously celebrate the world and complain rancorously against death. In "The Beggar," for instance;

Curse the beggar in the street
    that he has less joy than I
    as at these fine old trees' feet
    body-satisfied I lie.

and

He has damned my fine-bound book
    and my pleasantness of meat

> blasted with his withering look
> all that once I glad could greet.

> Curse the beggar in the street
> curse the beggar that he die . . .

This reluctant surrendering of pleasure compares with Horace's
Odes I, xxxviii:

> I hate the Persians, boy, and all their ways,
>   Their chaplets tied with bark I cannot stand.
>   Stop your investigations in what land
> Lingers the last rose into autumn's days.

> Add nothing to the wreath of myrtle made;
>   No more I care for; and it well suits you,
>   My slave, the myrtle, and I think me too,
> Under a thick vine drinking in the shade.[14]

Horace's Ode "To Dellius" (II, iii), in a more chastened mood,
is perhaps closer to Mason. There "cups of the best Falernian
wine" are set against the knowledge that "some day you must
die":

> Rich man and beggar alike, we are all
> To one place driven; soon or late the urn
> Throws out the fatal lot for each in turn
> Which sends us to the boat with no recall.[15]

A certain homogeneity of tone and attitude in Mason's work
may suggest itself here. If this Horatian ode finds a responding
chord in "The Beggar" it equally does so in "After Death" and
many other poems. Horace's gentler aspect is lacking. As a
momentary stay against death-knowledge, Horace can call upon
real possibilities of peace and enjoyment. About Mason's "slight
pleasure" hovers a growing and vitiating guilt-feeling. The urge
to evade the idea of death causes him, in some poems, to contrast present harshnesses with the myths and culture of the past.
    More than once he uses his sense of the Roman Stoics' world
by inverting their conceptions of life, as *Odes* III, xxx:

> A monument more durable than brass,
> Rising above the regal pyramids,
> Have I erected . . .[16]

is inverted by "The Lesser Stars":

> We are they who are doomed to raise up no monuments
>   to outlast brass:
>   for even as quickly as our bodies' passing hence
>   our work shall pass
>   of us shall be no more memory left to any sense
>   than dew leaves upon grass
>   there will not be even the least word of our eloquence
>   no one will cry 'Alas
>
> Alas alas for his too-swift passing away
>   he of the mighty thought
>   even before the slight sands of his poor flitting day
>   were fairly out:
>   oh could he have but lengthened a short year his stay
>   maybe then he'd have wrought
>   greatest things as the westering sun gleams with one
>   brightest ray
>   near setting and cloud-caught.'
>
> Such words can never be ours we know, yet we not complain
>   but hold high heads: it's meed
>   enough to have laboured and loved the labour we feign:
>   more, we make it our creed
>   that to bring our small tribute of incense leave others
>   to reign
>   is enough: yet indeed
>   at times we mind how we shed our best blood but to
>   leave not a stain
>   then truly our hearts bleed.

A curious parallel may be found between Horace's Ode "To His Bottle" (III, xxi) and Mason's sonnet "The Spark's Farewell to Its Clay," I.[17] Horace's tone in addressing his bottle is familiar and easy, while Mason's is supercharged with bitterness and regret. Mason's irony is raw and direct, Horace's subtle. In

Mason the same tragic sense of life is more assertive, and there is a strong sense of soul which goes beyond the Horatian mood:

> Well clay it's strange at last we've come to it:
>   after much merriment we must give up
>   our ancient friendship; no more shall we sup
>   in pleasant quiet places wanly-lit
>   nor wander through the falling rain, sharp-smit
>   and buffeted you, while I within snug-shut:
>   no longer taste the mingled bitter-sweet cup
>   of life the one inscrutable has thought fit
>
> To give to us: no longer know the strife
>   that we from old have each with each maintained:
>   now our companionship has certain end
>   end without end: at last of this our life
>   you surely have gained blank earth walls my friend
>   and I? God only knows what I have gained.

Another classical source of "The Spark's Farewell" is the emperor Hadrian's dying address to his soul. Aware that it is leaving him, he wonders for what bare place it is bound and bids it to be as light-hearted as it once was:

> Animula vagula blandula
> hospes comesque corporis,
> quae nunc abibis in loca
> pallidula rigida nudula?
> nec ut soles dabis iocos!

Mason's "The Young Man Thinks of Sons" could well have as epigraph the closing lines of Horace's Ode "To the Romans" (III, vi):

> What is it withering time does not abate?
>   Our fathers' age, worse than our grandsires' days,
> Bare us still worse, soon a more profligate
>   Posterity will take our wretched place.[18]

Many more correspondences can be found, for example between Catullus vi and Mason's "Flattering Unction," between Mason's "Vengeance of Venus" and many moments in the Roman love poets (in Propertius, but especially Horace's Ode "To Venus" — IV, i). Enough parallels have been drawn to show the pervasiveness of classical influence.

CHAPTER FIVE

Sad Mortality

Man's Longing for Immortality

IN a series of propositions in Part III of the *Ethics*, Spinoza suggests that the individual human mind endeavours to persist for an unlimited time, and he concludes, "The idea which cuts off the existence of our body cannot be given in our mind, but is contrary thereto."[1] Man knows, by observation and experience, that his kind is not immortal, yet in some sense he cannot believe this of himself and it is of his nature to try to live forever.

A most valuable work through which to see Mason's death-obsession is Unamuno's *The Tragic Sense of Life*, a treatise on Western man's hunger for immortality. Commenting on Spinoza's formulations mentioned above, Unamuno says:

. . . the longing not to die, the hunger for personal immortality, the effort whereby we tend to persist indefinitely in our own being, which is, according to the tragic Jew, our very essence, . . . is the affective basis of all knowledge and the personal inward starting-point of all human philosophy.[2]

This is very true of a stoic, mystical poet such as Emily Dickinson, a poet for whom death and immortality were foremost preoccupations and main themes. For Mason it is certainly so, that man's mortality is "the affective basis of all knowledge," but if it leads him to a "philosophy" it is at once elementary and ruminative.

"After Death" is the poem of a young man, totally engaged
in his own sense experiences. Each heavily-stressed item in the
list of sensual delights reaffirms simultaneously his celebration
of the physical world and knowledge of his own mortality. The
refrain of each stanza, the repeated phrase "but not for me," is
itself the death sentence. Here is demonstrated a main characteristic of "the tragic sense of life," our recognition that the
poet longs neither for immortal fame nor for a future life of a
different nature. He longs to continue, *as himself*, in this life.
The desire is youthful, vigorous, celebratory. Here is a sensibility
quite alien to that Swiftian irony which pictures the immortal
Struldbrugs encountered by Lemuel Gulliver on his disillusion-
ing voyage to Laputa.

In the following poem, "Old Memories of Earth" (*CP*, p. 28),
Mason opens with a statement pondering his lack of belief in a
future life, another world to which we are carried after death:

I think I have no other home than this.

Death then, means complete annihilation. Characteristically, he
has a strong sense of the past, which he can feel and visualize.

I think I can recall
back even past the time I started school
or went a-crusoeing in the corner pool
that I was present at a city's fall.

It is an irony that his sense is "not only of the pastness of the
past, but of its presence," yet he cannot imagine any existence
of himself beyond his physical death.

His conviction that physical death means annihilation is
brooded on again in the Horatian "The Lesser Stars" (see above,
p. 61). The emotional charge of that poem comes partly from
the use of line-length—long balanced cleverly against short—
and partly from the choice of images—the present is evoked in
the language of transience and brevity. Concluding that it is of
no great importance whether or not one raises up "monuments
to outlast brass," the poet seems to imply that even temporal
fame is a desirable form of immortality. Greatness and power are

not of themselves important, but what is important is that *something* of each one of us should remain.

Certain features of this poem are puzzling. Undeniably the ground-base of it is regret at the mutability of human existence. Yet the tone of the opening may well carry a hint of negative irony, as if the poet had in mind also the phrase "sounding brass" from *Corinthians* (II, xiv. A.V.). This impression is reinforced by the employment of "stain" as a rhyme. Is this, then, a savage moment, close in spirit to the negativism of "The Young Man Thinks of Sons"? That cannot be answered with confidence. The problem itself (if indeed it is one) is a small token of the intuitive, rather than the intellectual nature of Mason's talent.

As a thinker, he does not seem to move in any direction. Smithyman has described him as "tender-minded," but this is altogether too simple. When Curnow speaks of Mason's "condition of shocked faith" we may accept this as a recognition of Mason's belief in life itself combined with his continuing strong sense of human mortality. As Wallace Stevens says, "It is the belief and not the god that counts."[3] To Mason the question of belief in immortality is much more important than that of belief in God or any god. It would very likely have troubled him as much had he professed atheism. The point here is not a matter of mind at all, but of temperament.

"Tennysonian Undertow" and Shifting Currents

Yet, over the years, there is some shift in mental attitude. A note which was to become more common in his work of a few years later occurs in "In Perpetuum Vale" (*CP*, p. 31), when he proclaims angrily against the way,

> wrathfully the sods have used
> this poor mouldering flesh of mine
> that I fool once thought divine . . .

A "Tennysonian undertow" has been remarked in his poetry and, while the title of this poem evokes the tragic immediacy of Catullus's eternal separation from his beloved brother, the central connection is with Tennyson's "The Lotos-Eaters." The "mouldering flesh . . . once thought divine" is at last disillusioned and, after the heavy and repeated burdens of human life,

> Bruised bruised bruised bruised
> . . . .
> bitterly the bleak sods fell

> I no hint of asphodel
>   amaranth ambrosia moly
>   paradise nor heaven holy
>   after these long pangs have found
>   but the cold clutch of the ground.

In Greek mythology, the asphodel is peculiarly the plant of the dead (with a possible implication here that there are no "dead" creatures, only death itself); amaranth is the never-fading flower of fable, emblem of immortality; ambrosia, food of the Greek gods, confers everlasting youth and beauty (lacking any "limit" of it, he may lack not only the immortality it endows but belief in the gods which are associated with it); moly, the herb given by Hermes to Odysseus as a countercharm against Circe, was to prevent him from being changed into a swine, a soulless creature.

> Mocking fell priest-benison
>   my poor rotting soul upon
>   scornfully their hope they flung
>   like a taunt their hymn was sung
>   'soon the rending of the tomb'

> Heard it I who knew the doom
>   I who knowledge-cup had quaffed
>   with unwavering lips then laughed
>   and with a wry throat I cried
>   voiceless because I had died.

The ministrations of priests have mocked him in not preventing him from taking the knowledge-cup (like Circe's cup) which had made him a mortal creature. This "knowledge-cup" corresponds to:

> that enchanted stem,
> Laden with flower and fruit, whereof they gave
> To each . . .

in "The Lotos-Eaters."

Tennyson's poem is curiously ambivalent. Its conclusion:

> Surely, surely, slumber is more sweet than toil, the shore
> Than labour in the deep mid-ocean, wind and wave and oar;
> Oh rest ye, brother mariners, we will not wander more.

suggests, on the one hand a death-wish and on the other a desire to evade death:

> ever to seem
> Falling asleep in a half-dream!
> To dream and dream, like yonder amber light,
> Which will not leave the myrhh-bush on the height;
> To hear each other's whisper'd speech;
> Eating the Lotos day by day. . . .

We can now bring Mason's poem even closer. Stanza VII of the Choric Song of "The Lotos-Eaters" opens:

> But, propt on beds of amaranth and moly,
> How sweet (while warm airs lull us, blowing lowly)
> With half-dropt eyelid still,
> Beneath a heaven dark and holy,
> To watch the long bright river drawing slowly
> His waters from the purple hill— . . . .

Four lines from the end of the poem, those who live and suffer and perish and escape the pains of hell to reach the "Elysian valleys" are seen as,

> Resting weary limbs at last on beds of asphodel.

"In Perpetuum Vale" may be read as a reply to, or consideration of, "The Lotos-Eaters." None of the magical plants is given to Mason's protagonist, who in "the cold clutch of the ground" has no companions comforted,

> To hear each other's whisper'd speech,

but is

> voiceless because I had died.

Both aspects of Tennyson's ambivalence are rejected, though the contrast deepens the irony in Mason's poem. The conviction of death's finality is also used ironically here to suggest his view of God.

Chance and Purpose

Sometimes he achieves a gnomic effect, as he does in the Blakelike simplicity of "Body of John," by the subtle alternation of contrasting lines:

> Oh I have grown so shrivelled and sere
> *But the body of John enlarges*
> and I can scarcely summon a tear
> *but the body of John discharges*

> It's true my old roof is near ready to drop
> *But John's boards have burst asunder*
> and I am perishing cold here atop
> *but his bones lie stark hereunder.*

Its ambiguity makes this a memorable poem. John's situation seems preferable to that of the "I" until the final word of the first quatrain, "discharges," reveals to us that John is a carcass, that what he discharges are the excrescences of decaying flesh, his bodily remains. Irony is reinforced by the opening of the second quatrain, when the "I" admits that *he* is on the point of death. In using the image of a dwelling-place for both John and "I" the poet has drawn attention to similarity as well as difference in their situations. The mild colloquial usage of "perishing" in l. 7 extends this, and, within the phrase, the exten- sion of "I am perishing" to "I am perishing cold" is cumulatively ironical. But the ultimate irony is that, apart from the contrast (between John and "I") not being as absolute as it seems, chance might well have seen to it that their positions were reversed.

This sense of chance in human existence is pervasive in Mason's work and is the basis for the "Miracle of Life" sequence, which is composed of two sonnets and a concluding poem of eighteen lines, loosely related. As it opens, Mason demonstrates his characteristic ability to look back into a far past or, as Stead puts it, "to reconstruct in poetic form . . . primary acts of self-consciousness."[4] Tracing his life-stream back "through times of cave of flint and bronze and fur," he considers,

How little did it need to end it all.

Survival and even propagation are by chance, thus making every incident and object in time a "miracle," including the soul, "the body's chief." This sense of miracle might well have confirmed in him a traditional belief (in a Creator, and therefore in man's purpose and possible immortality). He has lost whatever will he had towards such a belief, and the closing lines of the second sonnet—

for there is nothing by man known or guessed
that's not miraculous beyond belief—

allow for a possible ambiguity in the concluding three words. Behind his attitude to life and death is a passionate longing to know the *purpose* of human existence, but it is intuitive rather than rational. He could not say, with St. Augustine, "I believe in order to understand." Instead, it is quite consistent with his temperament and cast of mind to follow this poem of celebration, and conclude the sequence with a third which is a cry of despair at the determinism, "the bondage," which governs man's life.

When he prays:

Let me forget I am nothing but a mote
upon a mote that scarcely is more great

a grain of dust upon a tiny rote:
let me be thoughtless how I am now by fate

Being blind mad impotent as a wind-straw whirled
about guideless but by hope and despair
and am to be for unknown time and reason hurled
from dim-guessed world to world I know not where:

I impotent oh even to wish soon find
to cry "forget" serves only to remind

this seems not so much "shocked faith" as pessimistic agnosticism.
It would be easy to conclude there, but to do so would be to
ignore the positive sense of miracle in the second poem. Grief
here is for all kinds of limitation—a bondage to time in
particular. The mystery of man's fate and his powerlessness is
that he can never know the measure of his allotted time. By
implication this is the negative face of the poet's celebration
("I impotent oh even to wish . . ."). What grieves is not life
itself, but first and last the knowledge that we must die, wish
what we may.

Despair for human mortality is the dominant theme, virtually
all-pervasive, of *The Beggar*, in which "Miracle of Life" is
included. Later in this small collection similar preoccupations
are evident in the two sonnets, "The Spark's Farewell to Its
Clay":

What if my body has at its commands
strength beauty knowledge rule of many lands
still is not any hope that it can live.

A momentary hope, expressed in terms very close to orthodoxy,[5]
is considered, but rejected:

Perhaps I seek myself and am not whole:
times think I in some pure place there can wait
a far surpassing fellow for my soul
and joy to think when I shall find that mate—
still you good easy earth must pay earth-toll
I recollect and so am desolate.

The better-known first sonnet is one of Mason's most successful poems, a dramatic evocation of the moment of death when
soul and body separate. Sometimes Mason appears to believe
man has a soul, sometimes not. The traditional term "spark"
may be used here intentionally to avoid raising the whole
problem. At any rate the very question, the very doubt, is
exploited as a means of resolving the sonnet on a note of tragic
ambiguity (see above, Ch. IV, p. 62). The culminating question
here and its equivocal answer amount to: what is the purpose
of this life, all its sensitivity, all its richness of experience, when
it seems to end only in death? Yet we must notice that life
itself is an affair of "much merriment" and, though "bitter-sweet"
and a continuous "strife," of "pleasant quiet places" and
"companionship." Death's eternity and the apparent purposeless-
ness of life are summoned in the one phrase,

> now our companionship has certain end
> end without end.

Fame as Immortality

In his chapter on "The Hunger of Immortality" Unamuno writes
that,

> When doubts invade us and cloud our faith in the immortality
> of the soul, a vigorous and painful impulse is given to the anxiety
> to perpetuate our name and fame, to grasp at least a shadow of
> immortality. And hence this tremendous struggle to singularize our-
> selves, to survive in some way in the memory of others and of
> posterity.[6]

Mason's epigraph to "Herostratus at Ephesus," from Quintus
Curtius, gives the classic instance of this longing "to grasp at
least a shadow of immortality":

> The temple of Diana in Ephesus was burnt to ashes . . . by a
> profligate villain, who confessed that he had no other object in doing
> it but to preserve his memory. (*CP*, p. 39)

Later, Unamuno enlarges on his theme, describing "the longing for immortality, if not for substantial and concrete immortality, at any rate for the shadowy immortality of the name" (p. 70) as *erostratism.*

Tacitus (in his *Annals,* IV), gives a long account of such an aspiration on the part of one Cremutius. Herostratus's longing is derived from envy of his more renowned fellows (in a sense it is like Cain's envy, a misguided desire for divine recognition). To achieve posthumous fame Herostratus is willing to give up everything of this present life to become notorious rather than "be swallowed up, remembered not." As a result of his *acte gratuite* he claims, addressing the "ephemeral ones,"

> though you scorn me yet
> this outcast reviled mocked and despised fool
> alone inherits immortality.

Three poems in *Penny Broadsheet* are related to the theme of death and immortality. "Song of Allegiance," though it may seem conventional and unsophisticated when put alongside such a piece as John Crowe Ransom's "Survey of Literature," has a value and strength of its own and balances finely, in point of view, against the implicit nihilism of "Herostratus at Ephesus." Immortal fame is considered in terms of "the mighty minds of old . . . ," in particular the poets (and the list gives us an insight into those whom Mason found important to him at that point). Again we are forced to conclude that his pessimism engendered by death-knowledge is matched by a life-affirming vein. The effective contrast is made quite explicitly:

> Shakespeare Milton Keats are dead
> Donne lies in a lowly bed
>
> Shelley at last calm doth lie
> knowing 'whence we are and why'
>
> Byron Wordsworth both are gone
> Coleridge Beddoes Tennyson
>
> Housman neither knows nor cares
> how 'this heavy world' now fares

> Little clinging grains enfold
>   all the mighty minds of old . . .
>
> They are gone and I am here
>   stoutly bringing up the rear
>
> Where they went with limber ease
>   toil I on with bloody knees
>
> Though my voice is cracked and harsh
>   stoutly in the rear I march
>
> Though my song have none to hear
>   boldly bring I up the rear.

"Sonnet of My Everlasting Hand" (*CP*, p. 48), from the same small collection, comes of an impulse similar to "Miracle of Life," I. Where the latter is worked out in quasi-historical terms, in the present poem the imagination ranges geographically. There are weak points in the octet, such as the epithet in the phrase "the seething Spanish land," and the lines have been carried through by dramatic generalization rather than exactness or penetration of language, but the sense of how close all human life is to nothingness, how everything depends on chance, is strongly evoked. "These atoms that now constitute my hand," have moved through space (Africa, China, Spain) driven or carried by elemental forces, from one person to another, apparently at random and with no relevance to wordly rank or status:

> They have grown old in change and interchange
>   and after long adventurings have come here
>   to house the mutable spirit of this strange
>   uncomprehended thing, at once their bier
>   and womb: for even now they long to range
>   again that midnight future which I fear.

The "everlasting" of the title suggests the tragic irony of Mason's attitude. For the hand, and the body of which it is part, is "everlasting" only as matter or energy. While the human longing for immortality may find reassurance or even resolution in the idea or expectation of immortal fame, it is not (in Mason's case) assuaged by the monist or pantheist notion of survival in the All, the Parmenidean oneness. Each of us longs for the survival and continuance of his unique and present self.

Another poem in the same group, "A Doubt," poses the question whether man's knowledge of his inevitable death is innate or acquired:

> I do not know
> > when I was told
> > that men must go
> > to glut the mould
>
> Oh was I told
> > or did I know
> > I must grow old
> > and earthward go?
>
> I cannot say
> > if youth knows or learns
> > that man the clay
> > to clay returns.

Stoic Mortality

Only about a third of the poems in *No New Thing* (1934) are concerned with this double question of death and immortality. In this book he is, in one sense, at the height of his powers, his view of life has broadened and other themes command his attention. His range of *ideas* has increased and developed considerably. This is shown, for example, in such a poem as "The Young Man Thinks of Sons" (*CP*, p. 60). Most frequently this poem is read as expressing a depth of pessimism verging on misanthropy:

> Did my father curse his father for his lust I wonder
> > as I do mine

and my grand-dad curse his sire for his wickedness his
weakness his blunder
        and so on down the whole line

Well I'll stop the game break the thread end my race: I will
not continue
        in the old bad trade:
I'll take care that for my nerveless mind weakened brain
neglected sinew
        I alone shall have paid

Let the evil book waste in its swathings the ill pen write not
one iota
        the ship of doom not sail,
let the sword rot unused in its scabbard let the womb lack its
quota:
        here let my line fail:

Let the plough rust untouched of the furrow, yea let the blind
semen
        stretch vain arms for the virgin:
I'll hammer no stringed harps for gods to clash discords, or
women:
        my orchard won't burgeon.

I'll take care that the lust of my loins never bring to fruition
        the seed of a son
who in his nettle-grown kingdom should curse both my sins of
commission
        and what I left undone.

Yet the *choice* asserted gives this the character of a stoic poem,
an overruling of fate. The phrase "I'll hammer no stringed harps
for gods to clash discords" suggests that the direction of life
is out of men's hands and man can influence it only negatively.
Yet what is wrong with life is not specified or even actually
hinted, except in:

I'll take care that for my nerveless mind weakened brain
neglected sinew
I alone shall have paid.

It is the aging, the process of decay, the inevitable progress
towards death, then, that is the cause of the young man's willed
negation.

Sex as Immortality

Obsession with immortality is linked, in several poems, with sexual experience. In the Shakespearean sonnet "Flattering Unction" (*CP*, p. 61), the juxtaposition is no more than that. The opening quatrain has a Catullian ring, but the poem's drive is very much that of "Herostratus at Ephesus." First women are evoked, in their "fragrant whirlpool of perfume" which "maddens" the *persona* of the poem, "the old vagrant." Then the poem's force is dissipated and a series of stock-responses (imitation of one of the moods of Shakespeare's sonnets) takes over:

> Then I recall how my eternal fame
> stands up too strong for Time to overthrow . . .

In the closing couplet we change key again, returning to the tone of the opening, but now heightened and forced home by the rhyme:

> There's balm for flesh, flesh that's alive and raving
> to smell and touch these girls, with a fiendish craving.

Thus, the second and third quatrains, the beck towards "eternal fame," are an affective evasion. Bombast, they are swept away by the livid "fiendish craving" of the flesh. Again present sensation is everything compared with the emptiness of posthumous renown.

Two other poems which make this link between sex and immortality are "Tight to thigh and lip to lip" (*CP*, p. 64) and "Nox Perpetua Dormienda" (*CP*, p. 69). In the first, the symbol of the cup of knowledge is used as in the earlier "In Perpetuum Vale." Both poems are appeals for the life of the body against the knowledge of eternal oblivion. Sexual experience is regarded as fulfilment. Catullus-like in mood, these poems establish a poignant contrast between the body in life and the rotting carcass meaningless in death.

Although not overtly concerned with death, "Wise at Last" (*CP*, p. 71) is another shift in Mason's attitude to human existence and to the idea of immortality. This new view, which

here appears for the first time, occurs in several later poems.
It is standing-down, an abdication:

> Long I sobbed at my task
> now I leave it undone
> to loll back and bask
> in the good sun.

This, the opening note, is asserted in the conclusion even more
strongly:

> I sit in the sun
> and take my rest:
> when all's said and all's done
> negation is best.

These lines' poetic validity has been questioned. There is certainly no development in the poem as a whole, merely a conventional tilt at business and the Press "barons," teachers and
preachers. None of this is convincing, any more than the poet
convinces us that he really believes it is the "wise of heart" and
the "good and strong" who are cast out. The real interest of
the pieces is in the sense of defeat they carry. There is no
attempt to *think*, either towards or beyond the adopted attitudes.
"Wise at Last" is an expression of temperament, suggesting that
the commonly held view of Mason's Stoicism is over-simple.

Stoicism to Nihilism

Two poems in *End of Day* (1936) reinforce one's sense that
some kind of inner surrender has taken place during these years.
As Stoicism, these poems convey, at most, a sense of the stoic
defeated. "New Life" is an ironic title for a poem not in itself
ironic:

> Before I found
> how it is ungainly
> to stand your ground
> and struggle vainly

> Have my assurance
>   that I have known
>   sweat streaked endurance
>   and screech of the bone
>
> I have stripped for the fight
>   I have stripped for the main
>   I have stripped for lovenight
>   I shall not strip again.

These, the first three of six stanzas, are a complete and satisfactory poem in themselves. The remainder has far less force and immediacy. We move to the banal "charged hordes" (the "hordes" are a repeated stock-response at this stage of Mason's career) and the I-persona is abandoned for two stanzas in favour of "captains of events" (reminiscent of Henley) all alike crushed by "Times stone regiments." There is also a modulation from asserted will, "I shall not strip again," to the determinism hinted in the concluding

> veins which, I pray, no flow
> of zeal may flood.

Considered at this point, there is more ground for seeing Mason's work purely as the expression of a pessimist, but this is a position at which he arrived, a negation of some celebratory instinct which had created the tension of his best earlier poems.

In the second of the two poems in question, "Fugue" (*CP*, p. 83), he speaks of escaping from one dead self to another, one dead life to another. Clinging to the notion of selves he hints, in the first part of the poem, at the possibility of transmigration, but ultimately his over-riding sensations are solipsist, on the one hand, and on the other a welcoming nihilism. Mid-poem is a characteristic gesture reminiscent of the hortatory flabbiness of claims on "eternal fame" etc. in "Flattering Unction." It is a cry in the dark:

> how can any soul endure
> where the whole ground is impure

> with its own dead?
>   I'll escape
> these charnel-clutches and I'll shape
> fresh selves under other skies:
> and where there new ghosts arise
> I shall drag away once more
> and from that dead-polluted shore.
>
> And so till the last mutation
>   puts an end to all migration
>   and I lie in that blank land
>   where Time cannot stretch his hand
>   and the future cannot daunt me
>   and there is no past to haunt me.

Even the "migrations" which are a kind of evasion in themselves, occur only that one "self" or "ghost" may torment the next. Such responses are barely more than visceral, a compounding of the Heraclitean tenet that "we never step into the same river twice" with a conviction that each step is predeterminedly "impure" and "polluted." Paradoxically, by the time he wrote "Fugue" Mason had come to wish for that which he most feared. However nervy and unwilling his apprehension of it was, the sense that "negation is best" had come to dominate him.

His extremest nihilist statement is in the sonnet "Away is flown each petty rag of cloud" (*CP*, p. 102), first published (in *The Auckland Star*) in 1929, and then out of print until it reappeared in the "Uncollected Poems" section of *CP*. He was apparently as attached to the sonnet form as Rupert Brooke before him. It would be difficult (and of little point) to prove a direct influence, but (rather like that between "In Perpetuum Vale" and "The Lotos-Eaters") there is a correspondence between this sonnet of Mason's and Brooke's sonnet "Clouds." Brooke's piece exemplifies a characteristic strength of his, conveying a sense of cosmic activity. This is a strength Mason shares, a point of similarity between them; but there is a blandness about Brooke's universe quite alien to Mason. Brooke's clouds, in the octet, press "down the blue night" in unending columns of "noiseless tumult." "The Dead" are introduced in the sestet, not identified with the clouds but likened to them:

> I think they ride the calm mid-heaven, as these,
> In wise majestic melancholy train,
> And watch the moon, and the still-raging seas,
> And men, coming and going on the earth.

In Mason's sonnet the clouds have gone from the sky:

> Away is flown each petty rag of cloud:
>   now there is nothing left but a scrupulous sky
>   peering down like the inside of an eye
>   upon a turgid brain where phantoms crowd:
>   gone now the sunset pageantry, keen proud
>   cold as a Damascus blade and clear and high
>   the blue vault stares: and yet it's all a lie
>   mere air with being by our eyes endowed.

> This is the life of man and this shall be;
>   of all our toil and skill and pride and hope
>   and hate and plotting and low and piety
>   there shall be no trace left in the world's whole scope:
>   a little while with godly foes to cope,
>   then pass like cloud-shadows in a blind sea.

Structurally, Mason has followed somewhat the same pattern as Brooke, though he has used the octet to clear the sky of clouds. Where Brooke compares the Dead (in his sestet) with clouds afloat and observing the doings of mankind, Mason has used the image of the cleared sky to carry his sense of man's passing without trace. Octet and sestet are juxtaposed in some apparent confusion. Firstly,

> it's all a lie
> mere air with being by our eyes endowed

may be a mere rejection of anthropomorphic fancies such as that in Brooke's "Clouds." On the other hand it could be read as asserting that the material world itself does not exist. Or that it exists only in some highly contingent phenomenal sense so that (in the sestet) our very selves are no more than "cloud shadows in a blind sea" (now described as "blind" where, in the octet, it had been posited as "peering down like the inside of an eye"). Thus we ourselves either do not exist or exist merely to contend with the mysterious "godly foes." So unsatisfactory a poem cannot be accepted as a key statement of Mason's consciousness, but it is an interesting illustration of how formidable his nihilism could be.

Far more conclusive, and a much finer poem, is one from the "late" selection, Recent Poems (1941). This is "Flow at Full Moon," one of his most beautiful lyrics.

Your spirit flows out over all the land between
    your spirit flows out as gentle and limpid as milk
    flows on down ridge and through valley as soft and serene
    as the light of the moon that sifts down through its
            light sieve of silk

The long fingers of the flow press forward, the whole hand
            follows
    easily the fingers creep they're your hair's strands that
            curl
    along the land's brow, your hair dark-bright gleaming on
            heights and hollows
    and the moon illumines the flow with mother of pearl

Beloved your love is poured to enchant all the land
    the great bull falls still the opossum turns from his
            chatter
    and the thin nervous cats pause and the strong oak-
            trees stand
    entranced and the gum's restless bark-strip is stilled
            from its clatter

Your spirit flows out from your deep and radiant nipples
    and the whole earth turns tributary all her exhalations
    wave up in white breath and are absorbed in the ripples
    that pulse like a bell along the blood from your body's
            pulsations

And as the flow settles down to the sea it nets me about
    with a noose of one soft arm stretched out from its course:
    oh loved one my dreams turn from sleep: I shall rise
            and go out

>and float my body into the flow and press back till I find
>its source.

A poem of acceptance, it completes the range of his attitudes and poetry on themes of death and immortality. Linked back to the early "Sonnets of the Ocean's Base," it also completes the whole cycle of his poetry. The early sequence's final sonnet ends with the moment of re-birth, when "after drear days I felt again the sun." Nearly twenty years on, this has mellowed to the closing cadences of "Flow at Full Moon":

>I shall rise and go out
>and float my body into the flow and press back till I find
>its source.

Death is accepted. Mason's sense of the past now includes a source, a beginning. The whole question of immortality is left open, put aside. His moving into the flow towards the sea can imply that he is willing now simply to return to the primal chaos. Alternatively, the sea may be the sea of life (with the intuition that death itself opens out to a new life, a kind of immortality). Against this, there is a hinted, faintly sinister note in the words "nets" and "noose." "The sea nets me" may suggest that death will be imprisonment, confinement, rather than a venture into a new life. "Noose" is a violent word to have chosen when the image behind it is the slow loop of a meandering river. "My dreams turn from sleep" may well imply that the sleep (the waking life it presupposes) is unreality and the dreams themselves are the reality. Following his vision of a world perceived through them, he is carried (voluntarily, for it is he who floats his body; voluntarily in the sense of willingly, acceptingly) back to the source and meaning of his love, his existence.

The strength of Mason's best poetry rescues it from the charge of self-pity. Romantic, dramatic, it is not the poetry of mere self-dramatization. For all his continual preoccupation with death, poems such as "After Death" and "Miracle of Life," II amply demonstrate his awareness that it is not his own introversion only, but a sense of the common objects of human existence, which makes the prospect of inevitable death so poignant. A poetry too much attuned to the implications of death would have a claustrophobic air, as many of Mason's lesser pieces unquestionably have. His best work, however, frequently derives a genuine tragic power from its evocation of *atque in aeternum, frater, ave atque vale,* of common moments which will be lost for all eternity, of the separation of human beings forever, and of the knowledge that no human emotion or aspiration can alleviate our mortality.

CHAPTER SIX

"A Condition of Shocked Faith"

Puritanism and Belief in Life

TWO epithets most commonly attached to Mason's poetry and personality are "puritan" and "nonconformist." Among the most incisive comments on him is Curnow's remark that "Mason's poetry draws strength from the effort to reconcile a belief in the human spirit with an obstinate will-enforced scepticism about personal immortality."[1] Chapter five, however, tends to show that Mason's reactions to the immutable fact of man's mortality, his thwarted longings for immortality, were in themselves involuntary. His scepticism of personal survival after death seems anything but "will-enforced," though patently his obstinacy and persistence are at the very foot of his melancholy.

In *End of Day* there is a new positive note,

> Get your machineguns manned
> for a new way of war . . .

but it is also a more superficial note than that characteristic of the earlier poems. Underlying the despair of *The Beggar*, for example, is a real sense that the poet is in love with the things of this world. If his work at any stage "represents a condition of shocked faith," that faith is in the beauty and desirability of the world itself and of man's relation to it. We can say with confidence that his is a belief in human life itself, a belief which he loses by the time the significantly-titled *End of Day* is published.

What, then, of his puritan temper? Such a disposition does not commonly sort well with an affirmative view of life. Several critics have detected in the very tone of Mason's poetry the baneful influence of a nonconformist religious background; at least one suggests that the troubled spirit of Mason's adult life is the outcome of a religion-dominated childhood. His own claim is that as a child he enjoyed complete religious freedom.[2] At any rate the poems, up to and including *No New Thing*, are firm evidence of a religious preoccupation. Our problem is to recognize the nature of this preoccupation in view of his apparent inability either to believe in, or to care for, the idea of an after-life.

Frequently the poems reveal an acute sense of sin, sometimes to the extent of seeming sin-ridden. Such a consciousness might fairly be described as "puritan" (using the term in its most general way), but the "puritanism" is often distinct from, even opposed to, professions of a specifically religious kind. In "The Agnostic," an early poem which stands second in *The Beggar*, he assumes that the sense of duty is characteristic of the human spirit ("am no undutiful clod but all a man"). He employs the idiom of the evangelical nonconformist, the "Christian soldier," in phrases such as "the fiery van," the Bunyanesque "valiant lance for truth," "unflagging sword," "bane and bitter ruth"; he declaims of "the hosts of sin" and compares men, who "root and grunt like hogs in mire," with the Biblical swine. This choice of language and attitude, however, is used to turn back upon itself. What proves predominant is the "levelling, rational" spirit, a sense of existence expression of which culminates in the doubts implied by the title:

> But where's the van what's truth what's right what's wrong
>   I can make out no more than you my song.

Just as later, in the memorable "Judas Iscariot," he exploits the idiom peculiar to a certain type of Englishman to characterize Judas, so here he uses the very language of the nonconformist to create ironic tension between the letter and spirit of religious belief. True, it is a muted irony, but it is there and is typical.

Dominant as are the twin themes of death and immortality in Mason's work, his poems concerned with immortality are not necessarily also religious. Pieces such as "After Death" and "The Lesser Stars" are, in effect, negative celebrations. Loss of pleasure in the world's good, a sense of his own inability to create work of enduring fame (or sometimes that an enduring work is no compensation for body's death)—these are the commonest concerns even in many poems which may at first reading seem more conventionally religious. In "The Lesser Stars," for example, the phrase "Jah's radiant sign" is a mere prop,—but it could suggest that whenever Mason is conscious of the possibility of God, he thinks of Him not as the Christian God of love, but as Jehovah, the Jewish God, God of Wrath. Such would be typical of the colour and caste of Mason's death-dominated mind. "Radiant" may suggest lightning quite as appositely as "celestial light." Perhaps the "shocked faith" is not so much that as doomed celebration. "Old Memories of Earth" (*CP*, p. 28) offers a somewhat different exposition of the agnostic view. As a poem, this gains in force through its apparent naivety. "I think I have no other home than this" may offer a denial of all life other than the present one. It may simply suggest a *doubt*. The phrase "I think" vouches, at one and the same time, for apparent doubt, for the poet's sincerity and, in its directness, for a naive view which gives us access to an honest tentativeness. Having no cognition or memory of other lands or other lives, the poem's *persona* yet leaves open the possibility of their existence. In line four, the phrase "these make out they have" hints at scepticism:

> Perhaps they have done will again do what
> they say they have, drunk as gods on godly drink,
> but I have not communed with gods, I think.

This passage again concludes with the reserving phrase, though there is an obvious technical need which may have dictated its use. Yet the remainder of the poem reads as if it were an attempt to explain a transcendent experience. The "fellow I have known" (the nature of whom is not described) *may* have been known in some former existence or in the present life on a non-rational plane. If this possibility is ruled out, there is no point at all in the "fellow's" presence. We must assume that he is there is an intuition of something, but we can go no further.

Visceral Christianity

At that time Mason was preoccupied with thoughts of Passion and Resurrection. In "The Vigil" (*CP*, p. 29) the persona plays the passive, listening role, involved in the drama through his feelings about it (such a stance is not uncommon in Mason's poetry). Much as in Edward Thomas's poetry, he is the melancholy observer, aware and apprehensive:

> Morning came and the cock crew
> clearly, shrilly and I knew.

All night long he has listened to the sound of the sea, and on the seashore, the edge of being, has heard men dig. Cockcrow suggests, as well as dawn, denial or betrayal. This *persona* has betrayed Christ, or it may be some sense of godhead in himself, by inaction. Fruitful ambiguity allows a parallel evocation of Christ's Passion with the lost innocence of the poem's *persona*. Characteristic as it is of the undisguised tentativeness to be found frequently in Mason's earlier work, the final sentence is more tangibly concise if we can assume ambiguity in the phrase "and I knew." Thus it might be taken to describe a state of forfeited innocence ("and I became more knowing"), but also the moment of revelation, when he realized that Christ had died for him.

Much could be built from such interpretations, but they are not always possible. Behind them is not so much a sense of consistent thinking or integrated contemplation as of oscillating emotions. The strongest, stablest and most persistent of these emotions, preoccupation with death, leads us to believe that, strong as it is, the religious sense in Mason has remained always a *sense* and is not developed into any systematic thinking. A gesture of Christian humility is made, for example, in stanza three of "The Lesser Stars":

> we make it our creed
> that to bring our small tribute of incense leave others
>   to reign
> is enough:

Compare this with the Anglican phrase, "my station and its duties." It is directly contradicted in the poem following, "In Perpetuum Vale." There, priests are described as scorners and mockers, the Resurrection as a false hope. Taken as a religious statement (rather than anti-religious), "In Perpetuum Vale" is Calvinist, determinist. It implies that, for one who has quaffed the knowledge-cup, the Resurrection is without significance.

Different kinds of irony and ambiguity pose problems in "Tribute":

> Christ Jesus came to my door
>   riding upon an ass
>   and though I am but weak and poor
>   I could not let him pass
>
> I called to him and bade him stay
>   and bade him pass my porch:
>   then though it was all brightest day
>   I lit my every torch
>
> Then I though I'm but weak and poor
>   and though I am but small
>   spilt all my wine upon my floor
>   wasted my unguents all.

Is the speaker a disciple, so convinced of Christ's divinity (or, let us say, importance to him) that he dispensed or abandoned all his worldly goods for His sake? Or is this a rejection of Christianity in the same spirit as the agnostic poems already discussed? We note that the poor man's light was wasted (the light of his spirit?) because, when he lit it, the time was "brightest day." Prodigality for love of Christ, is that the explanation? Wine and ointments, both, are wasted. The whole weight of the stanza (and, if we accept this interpretation, the poem) rests on the word "wasted" in the final line. Was all that wasted, then, which

was done for Christ's sake? Was it wasted because even Christ
could not bestow immortality on earth?

Sometimes Mason adopts a position which is definitely agnostic, at others almost atheistic. Often the agnosticism occurs in the
same poem as an expression of grudging belief. When this happens the belief is expressed ambiguously, tentatively, or ringed
about with complexities. We have noticed that, in the first poem
of the sequence "The Spark's Farewell to Its Clay," he is careful
to speak of "spark" rather than "soul." In the same poem he
makes a fairly conventional reference to "the one inscrutable"
whom he sees as having "thought fit" to create his situation. He
ends by denying implicitly belief in the resurrection of the body.
The phrase "God only knows" in the concluding sentence, if we
accept it at its cliché valuation, simply reiterates doubt that the
"spark" has gained anything whatsoever. Taking all of Mason's
other work into account, together with his limitations of thought,
this is the probable reading. There is, however, the peculiarity
that the phrase is not (as it usually is) used as an exclamation.
As it stands, there remains the possibility of accepting it as expressing some kind of faith in God. We could assume a *complete*
faith, but this certainly would not accord with Mason's attitudes
in other poems. The "clay" has gained "blank earth walls" as its
future. The "spark" may well have no future, but the sentence
could be read as an acceptance of what it has already gained
up to that moment. This conclusion which is not an exclamation
gives the poem its peculiar resonance.

Mason's own continuing uncertainty of what he really believes
lends most of his best poems a deepening ambiguity. "Miracle of
Life" I and II (*CP*, p. 33) are interesting in this respect. Discussed above in terms of Mason's preoccupation with immortality, certain other aspects of the two poems are relevant here.
II begins,

> Each day brings on its common miracle,

and concludes,

> for there is nothing by man known or guessed
> that's not miraculous beyond belief.

Here, even if the intention of "miracle" and "miraculous" is not theological, their context lends them a quasi-theological charge. Again there is a verbal ambiguity in the phrase "beyond belief."

"Miracle of Life," I (better known of the two poems) describes the life-process in evolutionary terms. The sestet ponders how little had been needed to stem the life-stream's flow:

> Miraculous how my life-stream has flowed
> from birth to birth down through each ancestor
> through times of cave of flint and bronze and fur
> when distant dam delivered of her load
> scarce guessed yet without whom I ne'er had trod—
> saw my old half-brute forbear smile at her
> and later saw him spring and lust and err
> and mate and spawn new sires in new abode
>
> How little did it need to end it all—
> a little venom here or there a cleft
> in one of many rocks or a cliff-fall
> an arrow one shade more to right or left
> some wound at any time however small:
> and this poor link of life had been bereft.

If there is any specific point in Mason's work which can be seen as manifesting a "shocked faith," it is here, as he contemplates the miracle of his own survival. He does not, however, reject the possibility that it is merely circumstantial, a matter of chance. Neither is it a matter of selection. He could have considered, for example, that other life-streams were prematurely ended which might well have developed into a race of saints. Ultimately the poem implies a celebration of the *common* life around him. That is the "miracle."

"Sonnet of Brotherhood" (*CP*, p. 35) is concerned with an aspect of his central theme, the simple fact of human suffering. His frequently repeated sense that to live is to suffer finds one of its more memorable statements in this poem. Fate hems in "these beleaguered victims this our race." It is everywhere, "on every side." All men are "betrayed alike." We are placed on a remoter edge of a universe whose very nature, even whose magnitude, we cannot comprehend. Combined with our sense of our mortality, we carry intuitions that this universe is hostile and dangerous to us and we ourselves are solitary within it. This sonnet is existentialist on more than one level. The "garrisons" are a figure for the consciousness of individual men, and the poem expresses the tension betwen man's fear of his own alienation and his need for brotherhood. Mason had not here, as he had in later poems, any gesture in mind towards international actualities, nor even national ones. Yet "Sonnet of Brotherhood" is undeniably relevant to the New Zealand situation, as subconscious expression.

We are now looking to any possible religious implications of the poem. C.K. Stead, in summing it up as "a statement of the human identity besieged by its foreknown doom, and of the naturalness of charity in the conditions of that universal siege"[3] has a point. The only remedy for the human condition is the contingent, existential one of brotherhood, wherein "friend and foe are friends in their hard sort."

Even "Herostratus at Ephesus" may be read as a poem with religious implications. It is on the solitary, the outsider. Phrases such as "mine is still the crown" are more truly appropriate to Christ than to Herostratus (who, after all, is no more than an arsonist). The parallel is inescapable and is typical of the reverberations set up by Mason's better poems. We can accept the "erostratism" conveyed as an ironical expression of human folly, but in our realization of Herostratus's delusions of grandeur is carried a knowledge, perhaps even a feeling for, the myth that Christ truly "inherits the kingdom" and, suffering His Passion, appeals to the human spirit or (at least) the human imagination.

While two poems of *Penny Broadsheet* explore the death/immortality theme the only directly religious poem of the group is "Oils and Ointments":

> Let me fall down about your feet O Christ
>   that have bruised and bled along the lonely way.
> wait here my bringing forth those highly priced
>   treasures I have saved up this many a day,
>
> The ointments I bring up to you my lord
>   gleam jewels like a steel-flashing beetle shard

lo! I shower down cascading the rich hoard
frankincense aloes myrrh cassia spikenard,

Sluggish oil that glints O look rainbows and gold
gently assailing unguents the orient has spiced
slow pouring balm smooth smearing calm behold
and stretch out your soothful longing foot O Christ.

This is unequivocally a religious, even a Christian poem. It has affinities with the earlier "Tribute" (discussed above). Both tell of a sinner's meeting Christ, Who is on a journey. There is no irony in the present poem. Here the poet dwells with a kind of sensuous delight upon contemplation of gifts and unguents. Mason was apparently fascinated by Christ's journey (or His entry into Jerusalem, perhaps). No hint of rebellion is here. Either the poem was written a long time before its printing or it shows yet another shift in a struggle between an obstinate, in-bred Christianity and an emotional scepticism.

No specific external evidence is available which would help to date this poem early, but it has resemblances of tone and image to the "Sonnets of the Ocean's Base," which offer at least the possibility that it was written before most work in *The Beggar.* The point is of interest. Even a casual glance at Mason's *Collected Poems* will show that he is steeped in Bible and scripture. A likely development is that he gradually moved away from Christian belief after adolescence, but without systematically thinking out his attitudes to it, i.e. that he became a "spiritual drifter." Yet, as we shall see, there are other possibilities. Some of his more positive religious statements occur comparatively "late" in his career as a poet.

Christianity as Myth

About one third of the poems in *No New Thing* may be read as religious in theme or intention. The introductory quatrains, "If the drink that satisfied," compare Mason's poems with the vinegar mockingly and yet mercifully given to Christ at the Crucifixion. This particular poem has been cited as an example of a growing self-consciousness in Mason's work, though "Song of Allegiance" could be regarded as a somewhat earlier example of such a trend. More directly interesting, in terms of religious statement, is the immediately following poem, "Stoic Marching Song" (*CP*, p. 54). Here the *persona* observes that "my soul is not to save," which may mean that he does not believe in "heaven" or in "salvation," although that would make it either irrelevant or inaccurate to say that he is "prey of doubt." Alternatively, "not to save" may be taken as "I shall not be saved (others will)." His speaking of "the gods" reveals a cast of mind moulded somewhat by classical studies. Unconsciously he appears to place the classical sense of gods on an equal footing with the Christian God and, similarly, in "Evolution" there are references indifferently to "gods" and "God." Perplexingly, a Christian reference occurs in the cliché "God knows what" (the phrase in "The Spark's Farewell to Its Clay").

"Evolution" is a typical expression of Mason's "doubt," posing the question, "If life has a religious purpose why is it not revealed to us?" To him, the possibility of our having been sent into this life for God's purpose and not our own is repugnant, extreme cruelty. A somewhat similar idea is expressed in "On a Dead Cripple," a poem which, although anthologized in the 'thirties, had not been included in a book before the *Collected Poems* (p. 101). There again is a simultaneous acceptance of God's existence and wonder about it.

Mason's three best-known poems, iv—vi of *No New Thing*, are in some sense religious. The first two, "On the Swag" and "Judas Iscariot," have religious subjects, the third, "Footnote to John II:iv," begins from Jesus's answer to Mary at the marriage at Cana. Clearly and simply, the emotional charge of "On the Swag" is pro-Christian:

> His body doubled
>   under the pack
>   that sprawls untidily
>   on his old back
>   the cold wet dead-beat
>   plods up the track.

> The cook peers out:
>   'oh curse that old lag—
>   here again
>   with his clumsy swag
>   made of a dirty old
>   turnip bag.'
>
> 'Bring him in cook
>   from the grey level sleet
>   put silk on his body
>   slippers on his feet,
>   give him fire
>   and bread and meat.
>
> Let the fruit be plucked
>   and the cake be iced,
>   the bed be snug
>   and the wine be spiced
>   in the old cove's night-cap:
>   for this is Christ.'

A mugginess, characteristic of much of Mason's less memorable verse, is absent here. There is a new authority and technical assurance while, at the same time, the mind behind the poems comes through to us precisely and economically. Christ is evoked as swagman, *clochard*, tramp, outsider. Such a figure may have been prompted by social conscience and the dour economic circumstances of the times, the immediate post-Massey era. It is not, of course, an unusual role for Christ, but it is a role of special relevance to the New Zealand imagination.

The solitary, the "man alone" is the only mythic figure to emerge so far from the New Zealand *pakeha* experience. This figure has always been related in particular to a sense of man's being alien to the New Zealand landscape. Critics and artists have, many times, attempted to describe this feeling of alienation, most successful being the novelist, John Mulgan.[4] "On the Swag" touches a chord in us for this reason, but it goes beyond the actual "man alone" figure to a recognition of community. Seen at a different level, it can be read also as a statement about the artist in our society, very much a man alone. Christ, the artist

and the solitary figure, merge. Christ and artist both strive to
make men more truly aware of each other, for only in brotherhood can a full life be lived.

"On the Swag" is an untypically tender poem. Consideration
of it brings us back to realizing Mason's inconsistency of thought.
We can arrive at no coherent "main line," and interpretation of
individual poems often depends largely on tone, on *how* one
hears the poems. Thus valuation is more than usually subjective,
and this may imply that, while one's own judgment is necessarily
limited it can sometimes be as authoritative as the poet's. A case
in point is "Judas Iscariot":

> Judas Iscariot
> > sat in the upper
> > room with the others
> > at the last supper
>
> And sitting there smiled
> > up at his master
> > whom he knew the morrow
> > would roll in disaster.
>
> At Christ's look he guffawed—
> > for then as thereafter
> > Judas was greatly
> > given to laughter,
>
> Indeed they always said
> > that he was the veriest
> > prince of good fellows
> > and the whitest and merriest.
>
> All the days of his life
> > he lived gay as a cricket
> > and would sing like the thrush
> > that sings in the thicket
>
> He would sing like the thrush
> > that sings on the thorn
> > oh he was the most sporting bird
> > that ever was born.

Here, as in "On the Swag," Mason has followed his instinct to dramatize. Curnow's observation that Mason has used the stance and idiom of a certain type of Englishman in order to characterize Judas,[5] usefully shows the poem's vividness and immediacy. It does not convince that the poem is necessarily a nationalistic gesture. Neither is it, in any direct way, religious. Yet is is a contrast to "On the Swag." Judas here is the antithesis of the Christ-figure, including the Christ-figure as artist. He is philistine, hearty, physical, hedonistic, upholder of the social conventions. He is a hypocrite, prime example of the truth that "one may smile and smile and be a villain." More than all this, he is the agent of death and, as such, an object of supreme horror. Yet his character and personality have been rendered with a sure wit, and the poem ends, with notable irony, on the word "born."

This is curiously "modern." Beside it the more popular and better-known "On the Swag" has a sentimental effect. What "Judas Iscariot" offers reaches far greater depths. Kendrick Smithyman has pointed out that in the late 'twenties there was in Auckland, under the guidance of Professor D.H. Munro, a group of Bergsonians. Smithyman claims that, following Bergson's theory of laughter, Mason habitually read "Judas Iscariot" as if the poem were, at bottom, a joke.[6] More commonly it is interpreted as portraying Judas as a nervy, hysterical hedonist. The range of possibilities seems greater still. The contrast between Judas's vitality and the gentleness of "On the Swag" is quite striking. Instinctively, the Judas poem is a rejection of heaven-sent nostrums. A note of triumph is held, as it were, in the poem behind the poem. The inescapable conclusion is there, that "the morrow/would roll in disaster" not only Christ but Judas himself. In the meantime Judas delights in his human existence. Because of the subject or focal point we are led, almost inevitably, to read "Judas Iscariot" as a gesture of ironic despair; but the dominant emotion is joy, elation. Such reverberations as these may be at the back of Dylan Thomas's admiration for it, the fact that he could quote it from memory and the question he put to Curnow, "Didn't that poem shock people in New Zealand?"[7]

How deeply religious such poems as "On the Swag" or "Judas

Iscariot" are it is hard to say. They owe a great deal to religious
associations in the common consciousness. Much the same may
be said of "Footnote to John" (*CP*, p. 58), except that its theme
of mother-rejection could be interpreted as dismissal of a kind
of life rooted in sectarian Christianity. Again we come upon an
absence of pattern, sporadic surges of faith alternating with
doubt and occasional violent rejections.

Other Religiously-Oriented Poems

Less successful and less well-known than these three poems is
"Ecce Homunculus," which immediately follows them and which
lacks their clarity and sureness of touch, seeming more akin to
earlier pieces such as "The Vigil," with which it shares an emotionally strident tone. Here Mason has difficulty with the form,
so that in mid-octet there is some momentary confusion as to
whether Christ or Pilate is being described. The poet seems uncertain what tone he should employ and so vitiates a tragic effect
with ironical references to "every righteous Hebrew" and "all
true zealots." Such a phrase as "he boldly went to die," with its
obvious lack of freshness, somewhat infects the remainder of the
sonnet. Reference to Christ's "soft flesh" (in itself a cliché),
weakens the poem in another way, the ambiguity of "soft."
Defects of "Ecce Homunculus" are dwelt upon here at some
length because they serve to demonstrate difficulties of interpretation regarding tone and vocabulary. These contribute to a
characteristic lack of clarity which throws the finest poems into
a contrasting high relief. In the sestet:

> And so he brazened it out right to the last
>   still wore the gallant mask still cried 'Divine
>   am I, lo for me is heaven overcast'
>   though that inscrutable darkness gave no sign
>   indifferent or malignant: while he was passed
>   by even the worst of men at least sour wine,

there is, for example, a suggestion of ambiguity about "brazened"
("brazen images," etc.); "brazened it out" means "faced it with
impudence, effrontery." An unsatisfactory ambiguity (i.e. obscu-

rity) in the phrase "gallant mask," could be a denial of Christ's divinity or, if as elsewhere[8] the idea of "mask" means acceptance of reality, quite the opposite. Otherwise, the phrase may have no overtones at all and be merely a cliché such as "kept his chin up." Lines twelve and thirteen are so phrased that the only sign to be expected from "that inscrutable darkness" is "indifferent or malignant." The malignance could be an expression of God's displeasure at men's actions, but what about "indifferent"? The words are so ordered too, that,

> though that inscrutable darkness gave no sign
> indifferent or malignant

contradicts, or cancels out, "lo for me the heaven is overcast."

Up to this point, then, doubts are cast on the divinity of Jesus and the responsibility of God in Heaven. This seems to be the poet's final attitude here, for he contrasts the indifference of Heaven with the reaction of *"even the worst* of men." That same phrase, whether consciously or not, is an affirmative note, rounding the poem off with a sense of man's effort towards goodness. The doubled qualification mutes it, but (through a diminuendo effect not unlike the conclusion of "Footnote to John") we sense an urge to celebrate the human in contrast to the heavenly.

Incidental Religious Elements

Some seven other poems are religious in preoccupation or have religious overtones. Three of these are in *No New Thing* and four more were first published in book form in the *Collected Poems*, although they were taken from manuscripts dated between 1924 and 1930. "The Young Man Thinks of Sons" (*CP*, p. 60) has been cited earlier for its Roman feeling and a certain affinity with the Odes of Horace. We may note here, in passing, that the young man considers human beings as instruments of fate or of the gods, victims of circumstance ("I'll hammer no stringed harps for gods to clash discords"). "The Just Statesman Dies" evokes sexual experience in terms of the Crucifixion:

And again comes back to me
    one holy day
    near the Feast of Crucifixion
    on lone cliffs I lay.

They were hands that held me
    far up towards the skies
    and their soft disdain
    of the sacrifice.

All day like a god
    with spirit transcended
    in warmth light and colour
    my senses were blended.

These stanzas bear some resemblance to an earlier poem, "The Vigil," but are in contrast to it. The phrase "like a god" suggests that the Feast of Crucifixion has been employed for its evocativeness rather than religious significance. What was very much a stricken feeling of betrayal in "The Vigil" has become no more than the means of an aesthetic or physical comparison. Behind this development there is a point of far greater moment. Through the *persona* or, rather, the subject of "The Just Statesman Dies," Mason outlines a contrast between a provident youth and an accepting or resigned old man. The just statesman's campaign for justice, learning, wisdom, his fight against Evil,—all these he comes to regard as vain. Two things only seem to him, in the end, fulfilment—walking in the cold night on misty hills and the "time well spent" when:

                one hot summer
        I lay with a girl
        more fragrant than cinnamon . . .

Thus we have a celebration of the things of this world in contrast to Man living always for the future. This is a peculiar gloss on the text, "take no thought for the morrow . . ."

"A Reality Prior to the Poem"

No New Thing concludes with a poem which exemplifies the occasional nature of much of Mason's work, "In Manus Tuas

Domine" (*CP*, p. 78). One may ask, what is "the reality prior to the poem" here? There is an incident of some sort, certainly, but its reality is thin. Specific references, to a period of nine hundred years, to the scimitars and spears, to pagan wars, may indicate that the poem derived from some single historical incident. If that is so it has not, in itself, had much force.

To digress for a moment, during the 'fifties and early 'sixties New Zealand poetry was thoroughly beset by an argument on what made a true poem. The most influential statement, for a long time, was to the effect that there must be "a reality prior to the poem" (a text adapted apparently from Wallace Stevens' assertion that, in poetry, both reality and the imagination are necessary, and indispensable to each other). In our context the "reality prior to the poem" theory was used to back up claims that the true New Zealand poem must be "local." (Thus seeming to follow Dewey and William Carlos Williams.) The term "reality" was accepted too readily as if it implied or meant no more than material or phenomenal reality. On such a criterion much of Mason's poetry must needs have been rejected had the confrontation been made. Later a related, though somewhat different, distinction clarified the whole situation. This was Owen Leeming's division of verse into poems of *flux* and poems of *event*.[9] Here a useful distinction is made between the generalized instinct to write poems and the genuine poetic event. What does not become clear, even in Mr. Leeming's intelligent summary, is that the "reality prior" to any given poem may be of more than one kind. This problem is discussed at length in Paul Valéry's essay "Poetry and Abstract Thought"[10] wherein the claim is made that the impulse to write poetry may be an impulse to use a form, a rhythm, to evoke an object or even to give expression to a feeling (which is not the same as merely to "pour out" one's feelings).

Returning to "In Manus Tuas Domine," we can now say that this is one of those poems, frequent in Mason, driven out of him by an emotion not clearly apprehended by himself. It can be compared with "Sonnet of Brotherhood," but here there are "faint-heart allies" instead of "friends in their hard sort." The "few devout" are loyal to Christ ("our steadfastness"), and it is pleaded that they, among the besieged, be saved from death. As an apparent plea for an elite it is untypical of Mason. It can be read simply as a plea against death itself, but the title is ironical and, in the closing two lines, pleas turn to curses:

> O Lord our Christ they are storming up the hill:
> curse you O Christ a continent they come.

Behind these curses is a positive sense of God together with the feeling that He could save the besieged if only He would, but, inscrutably, He does not. The curses come the moment before annihilation.

In "Lullaby and Neck-Verse" (*CP*, p. 110) and "Arius Prays" (*CP*, p. 108) we are given glimpses of Christ as Man.[11] The counterpoint of the former,

> Ah nestle down safe on your loving mother's knee
>   *There is not any hope*
> While Jesus watches over you, who died on Calvary
>   *A lank snake of a rope,*

implies that Jesus was Himself violently executed, that He could not help Himself and cannot now help the man condemned to be hanged. Arius wants to be assured both of Christ's immortality and of His Manhood, presumably because a man will understand the plight of all men and the impersonal gods do not:

> Oh do not pass them by dear Christ who think
>   that you were compounded in the common way
>   framed of impetuous blood and fallible clay,
>   that your body was made not to be saved but sink
>   down to the murderous grave, therein to stink
>   in foul corruption, on that evil day
>   by Golgotha—and your soul they say
>   drank with the rest annihilation's drink.
>
> Be with us Lord not only with our best
>   but when we mock your name and scoff and rail:
>   laugh with us like a man not like a god
>   a cruel god who gives death for a jest:

> be with us dead man when our feet halt and fail
> in that hard road your clumsy feet once trod.

The conclusion of "Nails and a Cross" (*CP*, p. 109)

> . . . while the troops divide my cloak
> the mob fling dung and see the joke,

has at once what one may call "proper" and "improper" ambiguity. The lines characterize the beast-like satisfaction of a mob witnessing the discomfiture of a fellow-being. Division of the cloak may suggest dismemberment or disintegration of the body. Christ's claim to Divinity to be "King of the Jews" may be the mob's joke. This is all conveyed through a "proper" ambiguity. The "improper" ambiguity is that the phrase "see the joke" can be taken to imply *the poet's* feeling that Christ's claim to be divine is a "joke." Consequently the phrase cannot properly be given to Christ although, in terms of the poem, this is unavoidable.

No doubt Mason is at times a religious poet, in the sense of having realized the historical force of Christianity. He is shocked and moved by Christ's Passion and by the Fall of Man. Whether or not he can be described as having faith is another matter. We have seen how, very early, in poems such as "The Vigil" and even "The Agnostic," he is emotionally disposed towards Christian faith. The closing couplet of "The Agnostic" shows a rational streak which vitiates his will to believe. For, as Unamuno says, "From whatever side the matter is regarded, it is always found that reason confronts our longing for personal immortality and contradicts it. And the truth is, in all strictness, that reason is the enemy of life."[12] Mason's attitude to Christ is everywhere equivocal because, driven to regard Christ's life and being as extraordinary, he returns over and over again to the feeling that a God of Mercy would not permit human suffering and death. An impulse of genuine religious involvement in his earlier poetry is already scarred by doubt. When we come to his finest poems on religious themes the religious or scriptural element is merely part of the background. The poems themselves are dramatizations of other aspects of the human condition, mother-son relationship, the artist in society, betrayal of brotherhood, "man alone." By now, it seems, Mason has become detached enough from the religious experience to use it for other purposes.

At times he appears to believe in, and fear, the God of Wrath; at others he speaks of "God," "the gods," "gods" indifferently. He could not reconcile the fact of death with the idea of a merciful God. His fear of death shocked him first to questioning and finally to becoming indifferent to religious "faith." He became resigned to the idea of his own death by the time he wrote "the beautiful and subtle *legato* of 'Flow at Full Moon,'" but there is no hint there of Christian faith. Acceptance goes no further than the stoicism of resignation to natural forces.

CHAPTER SEVEN

The Sense of a Universe

A T this point we have a number of elements to put together. A sketch of the quality of life in New Zealand in the 'twenties and 'thirties, an outline of Mason's life and an investigation of his religious sense and his attitudes to death and immortality, together with an account of how his mind is permeated with the thought and poetry of the classical Roman world —if we bring these things into mutual focus, what kind of picture have we of R.A.K. Mason and his work? Why is he a writer of importance in the New Zealand context?

Neither answer is obvious. As we have seen, there are contradictory elements in Mason's work, a certain unclear quality in his thinking and, in his poetry itself for much of the time, even an incoherence. A number of literary and other influences upon him have yet to be discussed. Certain aspects of the work, the prose in particular—which is virtually all at the journalistic level —have still to be considered to make the surface picture complete. It is necessary, at this point to attempt to match up aspects of the work which seem, on the face of it, to cancel each other out.

Mason's "Universe"

We can tackle the problem on its broadest front by asking: What is his sense of the universe, or of his own universe? Sometimes he feels himself to be a mere atom disposed without plan, as though the universe were, in Heraclitus's phrase, "a dust-heap piled up at random." Sometimes he laments that he is "all fast in that great unrelenting mesh"—caught up in a conviction of universal determinism. At one moment he will grieve at his own isolation, at another he will seem happiest in a world without people. A keen sense of the dramatic is typical of his poetry, yet (apart from the "old cove" in "On the Swag," and the "sporting bird" Judas) his poems are populated by groups or abstractions. Usually, his drama is the working out of something within himself.

Imaginatively, he has a strong sense of the movement of being through time, and yet no sense of a causal beginning. His "miracle" is, in truth, his own inner reaction to the world of phenomena, so dotingly catalogued by Whitman:

> When I heard the learn'd astronomer
> When the proofs, the figures, were ranged in columns before me,
> When I was shown the charts and diagrams, to add, divide,
> and measure them,
> When I sitting heard the astronomer where he lectured with
> much applause in the lecture-room,
> How soon unaccountable I became tired and sick,
> Till rising and gliding out I wander'd off by myself
> In the mystical moist night-air, and from time to time,
> Looked up in perfect silence at the stars.

In Mason's imaginative world, no people other than the poet himself are involved in this miracle. The details of history are not to be wondered at, rather the abstract process, the long chain of being which has continued from a past before human memory up to those moments in time which are his own existence. This continuance from ancestors "scarce guessed" is, he is emotionally convinced, entirely at the mercy of chance, for the tiniest accident could have abruptly terminated the whole evolutionary process. Thus, although it does not come within his cognizance (at least in the poems), his very attitude is in itself accidental. In the end it is a subjective "miracle," that *he* should exist, that the universe containing him should. There is virtually no sense of linkage with other human beings, so that in a poem such as "Evolution" (*CP*, p. 55) the feeling of being an isolated victim of impersonal processes is very strong. Everywhere Mason apprehends the tragedy of human existence in terms of the wonder

and beauty of everyday life contrasted with its apparent pur-
poselessness. "Each day brings on its common miracle," it seems,

> for God knows what experiment
> of breeding men as men breed mice
> for scientific sacrifice.

Whereas here the world may be hypothesized as a heartless
experiment of mysterious supra-human forces, in such a poem as
"Old Memories of Earth" (*CP*, p. 28) the strong sense of pro-
longed continuity occurs again, but there again also the world
is empty but for the druid-like priests, and the mysterious "fellow." That whole poem conveys a solitary determinism, with the
solitariness itself enforced by the determinism. Where Mason is
at his most bleak is in calling up a world outside his own time
span.

His reiterated inability to imagine any part of himself surviving beyond present life makes his universe seem to us almost
entirely physical. In poems such as "The Spark's Farewell" or
"Sonnet of my Everlasting Hand" we are in contact with a world
where only one person, the poet, is real. An apparent indifference to other individual people finds its completest expression in
the paradoxical death-wish of "The Young Man Thinks of Sons."
In the conclusion of "Flow at Full Moon" (*CP*, p. 94) and in
"Sonnet of my Everlasting Hand" he approaches pantheism; but
for him the atomic, physical nature of the universe renders contemplation of death, "that midnight future which I fear," more
terrifying than ever because what troubles him is the inevitable
cancelling of our human individuality. This alone shuts the man
into his solitary self. Solitariness is a condition of Mason's world,
and therefore of his poems, but it is also a reflection of a strong
sense of man's isolation in the New Zealand environment at
least up to the beginning of the Second World War.

The combined notes of solitariness and determinism occur
again in "Sonnet of Brotherhood" (*CP*, p. 35). In conversation,
Mason has himself described this as a poem about "the state of
the universe." "Fate's gigantic plot" is human life itself, culminating in the gratuitous, inevitable cruelty of human death.

Whereas at heart Mason is a natural celebrant of worldly joys, the "brotherhood" is not a bond of brotherly love, but of hard necessity:

> Such men as these not quarrel and divide
> but friend and foe are friends in their hard sort.

Universe or Nation?

In one of his "Adagia," Wallace Stevens says, "The world of the poet depends upon the world he has contemplated."[1] Naturally, Mason's sense of the world is circumscribed by the fact that he has travelled very little outside New Zealand. Such travelling as he has done has been undertaken largely for purposes of political journalism. A question which arises naturally in connection with his work, then, is—how specifically "New Zealand" is it? What qualities of the work give it its peculiar value and relevance in the New Zealand context? As part of a search for national identity, both here and in Australia many artists have concerned themselves with concentrating on the search for nationally individuating gestures, attitudes, tones, flavours.

Mason is the least *deliberately* "national" of the writers of his generation. The other prominent poets, whose work dominated the New Zealand writing scene from the early 'thirties until the end of the 'fifties—Brasch, Curnow, Fairburn and Glover—have all been consciously (and at times militantly) New Zealanders in their approaches to life and poetry. Charles Brasch, after nearly a decade away in Europe (including the Second World War) returned to found, and to edit for twenty years, *Landfall*, the most substantial literary journal New Zealand has ever had, notable for its intellectual probity and consistently maintained good standards. Denis Glover, something of a wartime hero in Europe, is also forthrightly the New Zealander. His nationality pervades both his work and his public presence. The late A.R.D. Fairburn wrote continually and extensively in a dedicated attempt to improve the quality of New Zealand life, while Allen Curnow constantly attacks the assumption that it takes "overseas experts" always to solve our problems for us. Alongside all these, his contemporaries and associates in the lonely enterprise of being an artist in New Zealand, Mason (who has spent less time away from his country than any of the others), is least assertively the "New Zealander." What, then, is one to think of his leading statement in the notes to *No New Thing?*—

> Some of these poems were intended to appear in a vast medley of prose and poetry, a sort of Odyssey expressing the whole history of New Zealand.[2]

Remembering the classical colouring of Mason's mind, such a statement could be dismissed simply as "a way of putting it," with the observation that he had his mind on the Odyssey rather than on New Zealand. This would be too easy a dismissal. Considering the full range of his work, one will uncover little *prima facie* evidence showing him as a writer especially conscious of his nationality or of his country as a geographical region. With the work of Kendrick Smithyman and Keith Sinclair, in the late 'forties and 'fifties, we have a conscious Auckland regionalism (which, even so, was not "nationalist" in intent). Vast importance was attached to a consciousness of New Zealand history, and the conditions which produced it, in the early work of Curnow and (to a lesser extent) of Denis Glover. Discovering images of pain and severity in geological form and process, Charles Brasch has drawn his symbolism from the natural landscape of these islands. Fairburn's longer poems are largely records of his reactions to local scenery and New Zealand history.

In all these poets is a sense of their "taking thought" which is almost entirely absent from Mason. Nothing as extensive and systematic can be traced in his work; but, if he was not specifically and consciously a "New Zealand" poet, he was so incidentally and naturally. Time and again we come upon phrases of his, fragments of thought when he is absorbed in what is his largest, and almost his only, subject—immortality, which are those of a spirit fully, though not self-consciously and often not concretely, alive to his local habitation.

Many of his most direct poems afford levels of implication which reveal a mind more complex than appears upon first en-

counter. In "Old Memories of Earth," for example, we were able
to discern agnostic religious attitudes, observing that the poet
begins by pondering:

> I think I have no other home than this
> . . . . . I have never any memories such
> as these make out they have of lands of bliss.

While the whole poem is an inward debate on the possibilities
of immortality and of after-life, this opening can quite validly be
interpreted and claimed as an unconscious declaration of national independence. Indeed, the second quotation might well be
an ironical comment (we have observed that Mason is not in-
capable of irony) on the garrulities of returned travellers.

In the early "Wayfarers" he accomplishes the difficult feat of
mingling Maori, English and classical names and allusions, making them all fit naturally into context.

> That I go out alone to them it seems
>   because they see none with me in the way
>   ignorant that the fabric of my dreams
>   are less intangible to me than they
>
> Ignorant that I have heard and seen Christ break
>   the bondage of his tongue-tied sightlessness
>   have walked with firm-faithed Mary to the stake
>   and kissed the hem of martyred Flora's dress
>
> And I in Lichfield frequently have been
>   Chatterton's accessory in suicide
>   have Gaius Marius in Minturnae seen
>   for many hours by Waitemata's tide
>
> Burnt Dian's temple down at Otahuhu
>   and slain Herostratus at Papatoe
>   and here in Penrose brought Aeneas through
>   to calm Ausonian lands from bloody Troy.

Only recently in some poems of the Maori poet, Hone Tuwhare,
is such naturalness repeated. Yet, although the New Zealand

names are there they are not the poem's chief point in themselves. Rather this is that the world of the imagination is both
solitary and universal, keeping no national nor universal boun-
daries. Thus no act of the imagination necessarily depends upon
the thinker's surroundings.

"Wayfarers" is not one of Mason's better poems even though
such varied elements are assimilated into it quite naturally. It
touches a point in his work where strength and weakness are
very close. Through imagination he claims the past and denies
his own isolation. Ultimately the gesture is a romantic one which
serves to highlight his own personal solitariness and, by extension, the solitariness of the New Zealander. Thus it happens that
one of Mason's dominant individual characteristics, his alone-
ness, is to be found writ large in the New Zealand temper, the
New Zealand imagination. It is a chief reason why his work
strikes such a responsive chord. That is the strength. Weakness
is in the implied possibility that a full creative experience can
be the product of introversion alone. It is always arguable that
this is so, but in Mason's case one can resolve the argument only
by pointing. His least satisfactory work is usually that which
makes no contact with his surroundings, but which attempts to
express emotional experiences merely in terms of his reading or
abstract thinking.

More distinctly and viably a New Zealander's poem is "Latter-
Day Geography Lesson" (*CP*, p. 40). Mason humorously substi-
tutes an Eskimo for Macaulay's New Zealander surveying the
ruined remains of "London in English times." It can be said, at
least, that the poem illustrates a certain detachment regarding
England and the "English" ethos:

> This, quoth the Eskimo master
> was London in English times:
> *step out a little faster*
> *you two young men at the last there*
> the Bridge would be on our right hand
> and the Tower near where those crows stand—
> we struck it you'll recall in Gray's rhymes:
> this, quoth the Eskimo master
> was London in English times.

This, quoth the Eskimo master
    was London in English days:
    beyond that hill they called Clapham
    boys that swear *Master Redtooth I slap 'em*
    I dis-tinct-ly heard—you—say—Bastard
    don't argue: here boys, ere disaster
    overtook her, in splendour there lay
    a city held empires in sway
    and filled all the earth with her praise:
    this quoth the Eskimo master
    was London in English days.

She held, quoth the Eskimo master
    ten million when her prime was full
    from here once Britannia cast her
    gaze over an Empire vaster
    even than ours: look there Woking
    stood, I make out, and the Abbey
    lies here under our feet *you great babby*
    Swift-and-short do—please—kindly—stop—poking
    your thumbs through the eyes of that skull.

His use of a particularly English idiom, a certain kind of English epithet in describing Judas (*CP*, p. 57)[3] as the "prince of good fellows," "the whitest," "the most sporting bird," who "lived gay as a cricket," may be read as a criticism, a rejection of British snobberies and British class distinctions. Can we go so far as to perceive in it a rejection of England? We should note that Judas was "with the others." Indeed, he laughed in company. It was *"they"* who described him (approvingly) as "the veriest prince of good fellows." The poem's New Zealand element could well be of a different order from a negative characterization of England. Judas's singing and sporting can be attributed as easily to a New Zealander as an Englishman. The idea of being "a sport" ("he was the most sporting bird") has more than one significance for New Zealanders. Mason uses "bird" elsewhere in a similar way, in the title of *This Bird May Swing*, where it has a contemptuous air. Anti-English the poem may be, but it could equally well be anti-sport, or paradoxically anti-religious.

More than one critic has noted the difficulty of discussing, or even describing, "Be Swift O Sun" (*CP*, p. 65). I would not myself have looked at it primarily for its New Zealand qualities, as Allen Curnow does. "An occurrence in nature," yes, but even more, for the poem has a feeling of trance about it, the inevitability of a somnambulist's walk. Curnow, however, sees it as "the most explicit admission by Mason that he inhabits a Pacific island." Earth's relationship to sun, the hemispheres of night and day, are connected with themes of separation, absence of the loved one and the possibility of her return over the sea. The sun sinks over the rim of the horizon and the poet sees last light on sails and ships' hulls. France and/or the whole Northern Hemisphere represents Dis, the underworld, both because in the light of his own world it is dark there and because there his love is held captive. "Those far alien ways" are, of course, the other side of the world, but this awareness of geographical situation does not argue, necessarily, for "the distinctively native-born character of Mason's poetry."[4] The "ways" may be alien to the poet simply because they are beyond his direct experience. He longs for her return, finding the light of day itself a useless thing without her:

> Here your labour is null
> and water poured upon sand
> to light up the hull
> which at dawn glimmers on to the land
>
> And here you in vain
> clothe many coming sails with gold
> if you bring not again
> those breasts where I found death of old.
>
> Why bring your ships
> from that evil Dis of a shore
> if you bring not the lips
> I kissed once and shall kiss no more.

Although not explicit, he is expressing an unbreakable attachment to his own environment. She has accepted the "alien ways" and he has not. Hence the desire for their meeting again, strong though it is on his part—for it alone would make the sun's coming meaningful—is recognized now as useless to him. Yet the poem in no way resolves itself. Feeling for both woman and land remains equivocal.

Most readily interpreted as a statement of "the poet as a New Zealander" is "Sonnet of Brotherhood" (*CP*, p. 35). It is not consciously so. That would have made it too self-consciously pseudo-allegorical. The sestet,

> And if these things be so oh men then what
> of these beleaguered victims this our race
> betrayed alike by Fate's gigantic plot
> here in this far-pitched perilous hostile place
> this solitary hard-assaulted spot
> fixed at the friendless outer edge of space,

particularly its three concluding lines, lends itself obviously to the "New Zealand" interpretation, perhaps especially to those whose thinking and feeling are still subconsciously British-orientated. Certainly New Zealand is more "far-pitched" from Britain than anywhere else with which it has a significant relationship. It is worth noting the similarity in intention between the words "pitched" and "flung," "far-flung" being at one time a common description of the British Empire. "Pitched" suggests also the idea of temporary settlement, as in "pitching tents" or "pitching camp." However, the sonnet's major charge derives from its cosmic relevance.

In a somewhat later poem, "Stoic Marching Song" (*CP*, p. 54), the poet speaks of marching

> to my grave
> through this hostile country here,

phrase and poem lending themselves more immediately to description as "New Zealand." Concerning "Sonnet of Brotherhood" the poet himself claims that the image of the beleaguered fort was intended as cosmic. This is of a piece with other poems such as "Miracle of Life" and "The Spark's Farewell to Its

Clay." Nevertheless, there are other reverberations. Here and elsewhere Mason speaks with profound relevance to the New Zealand condition.

"Song of Allegiance" (*CP*, p. 45) is his due acknowledgement that he is writing within the tradition of English poetry. It has more to say about longing for immortality and recognition of the exacting nature of his vocation than about nationality. Mason nowhere consciously attends to the task of being a "New Zealand poet"; yet he has rid himself of most of the baggage of poetry which is markedly English, except where he may use it for purposes of irony. All-embracing as it is, "Flow at Full Moon" (*CP*, p. 94) which at least momentarily resolves in itself every tension of the poet's life, may be regarded as his most "New Zealand" poem. The land, the woman loved, are one. Complete identification of loved and lover resolves the poem. The hint contained in that beautiful line of "Be Swift O Sun,"

those breasts where I found death of old

is here fully worked out. In the poetry as a whole, related *motifs* of mother-rejection and absorption-into-lover can usefully be read as rejection of "Mother country" and identification with the homeland.

The "Man Alone" Theme

Then there are those poems in which the central figure is the "man alone." This figure may have a double significance as New Zealander and as artist. The "man alone" or "*magus*" according to James K. Baxter, "by the performance of a symbolic ritual attains to forbidden knowledge."[5] Baxter places more emphasis on the "man alone" as artist than as New Zealander. Indeed, he continues,

Very likely the symbol of *Man Alone*, does not, in fact, reflect a morbid state of isolation from the European cultural tradition, but rather the condition of solitude essential for the performance of a ritual act. The anxiety, however, which accompanies the taking on of this role is a different matter. It seems to derive from the artist's awareness that his activity is regarded with indifference or even hostility by the society in which he lives. The symbol of *Man Alone* is thus objectified as the hobo, the social outcast, standing for the outcast energies, both criminal and creative, which the artist tries to reintegrate in his view of the world.

Distinguishing the artist from the people, he sees the "man alone" as a figure outcast, but goes on to show that "the myth of the isolated New Zealander is not of universal application. With the ordinary cultural background of an educated man, talent, and a mind alive to the meaning of his experience, a New Zealand poet need be no more isolated than one living in London or Greenwich Village." As statements of the artist's situation these are appealing, but some artists see themselves as the spokesmen for their society, and Curnow may have been voicing an unconscious objection to Baxter's idea of a private "ritual act" when he says of Mason's work: "The poems may be best understood—a New Zealander finds it easy to understand them so—as rituals of participation."[6] He supports this by drawing attention to Mason's use of plural pronouns in key passages.

The full significance of Denis Glover's "Arawata Bill and the old timers" of Mason's "swagger,"

> His body doubled
> under the pack

is that these were *of* the people. Their condition of solitariness is not meaningful only because the artist often claims to be isolated in a materialist society, but also because, whether they know it or not, the people are still a "confederation of hermits in the hills."[7] Applicable to the human situation as a whole, the "man alone" figure, as Keith Sinclair recognizes here, has a peculiarly historical validity for New Zealand. The social response to the hobo in "On the Swag" points towards Mason's hope, at that stage, of an existential goodness among men. Yet, intuitively, he has again touched upon a central fact about being a New Zealander. An existentialist, a religious, even a Christian poem—however we regard "On the Swag" (*CP*, p. 56)—it is certainly his most distinctive single contribution to the peculiarly New Zealand "man alone" theme. However, the figure, the idiom from which the poem's title comes, and even the theme itself, are no less typically Australian.

Baxter claims that, for an artist, New Zealand need be no more isolated than London or New York. The link he suggests, however, from one place to another is that of a common culture, and this is to minimize the special problems presented by any environment. Sometimes these problems make the "common culture" inadequate. A special feature of solitariness is that it is sometimes created out of the individual's cultural background. To be in a land whose historical associations are not one's own is to be isolated. The New Zealander's isolation may not be due to his geographical remoteness but to his lack of ultimate *rapport* with his own land. To return to Sinclair's "Waitara" for a moment:

> No people can possess a land,
> Where every single sod and stone is strange,
> And alien to the blood, who waits to oust
> The bone-cells, in the crucible of earth.
>
> We are all crucified in the earth,
> The earth our cross, exotic to our hands,
> We are all nailed by time's jest
> Who belong to the clayless climate of the mind.
>
> Ache in our back, O cliff before our mind,
> We cannot belong to you, nor share the peace
> That lies upon you like an incubus,
> For our loyalties are fathered in the mind.[8]

This sense of the peculiar qualities of a place is what gives such poems as Alistair Campbell's "Hut Near Desolated Pines" and "At a Fishing Settlement"[9] their immediate fascination. It is the main reason why Charles Brasch seems, of all poets, most profoundly a New Zealander. Sargeson has the same quality, and some of Baxter's own best early poetry is that in which the sense of place is strongest. In Sinclair it has become externalized and formalized as conscious regionalism. Mason, however, felt his isolation primarily as a sense of his own mortality. His sense of place is not particularly strong even though his sense of history is. Perhaps his feeling of isolation is reinforced, without his being aware of it, through factors in his environment touched upon by some of the later poets. Be that as it may, it goes beyond any consideration of nationality and deals in the simple, all-pervasive categories of life and death.

Mason's Herostratus is a "man alone," who may be seen as a type of the artist (or, perhaps, pseudo-artist). His action of burning down the temple of Diana is a "ritual act" representing destruction of the old gods, the old conventions. The conflagration is his work of art. Mixture of motives, disinterested creation of a work of art being combined with the longing for fame, is not uncommon; it is Milton's desire to leave "something so written to after-times, as they should not willingly let it die." This poem is at least as suggestive of the tensions between artist and society as is "On the Swag."

To say that Mason's poems are "rituals of participation" is to ignore perhaps too completely his romantic individualism. If his poems are not mere self-dramatizations, they are, at any rate, self-centred dramas. Sometimes the protagonists in the poems may choose not to participate (unless we regard rejection as a kind of participation). Social rejection of one sort or another is implicit in many, from "Wayfarers" (where he seems to reject the social world for a private one), to "Footnote to John II, iv," (*CP*, p. 58). Usually rejection is of a particular kind, however, as these two poems will serve to illustrate. An image, aspect or association of the society is rejected, but never the society as a whole. It must be true of any artist that he cannot reject his society as a whole, but only some element in it or facets of it. For this reason Baxter's interpretation of the "man alone" symbol is an incomplete one.[10]

The "outsider," the solitary, is appropriated to the New Zealand mythos in terms of the "man alone." As hermit, castaway, and so on, the "outsider" figure is common in Western literature of the past two centuries. Where it occurs in Mason it can only be added that this was a result of his private preoccupations and ruminations. All the elements of his vision which can be labelled "New Zealand" are there because they were in his bones and not merely in his mind. Perhaps his fullest, most complex and most objective statement of the "man alone" theme is to be found in "Twenty Sixth October," a poem made towards the end of his

two most poetically active decades. Up to this time he has
always conceived for himself a central role in life's drama
or some moment of life. He has identified himself with Christ,
with one isolated in some unfriendly corner of the world or
universe, as a restless spirit in a mortal body, as a tortured
frustrated lover, or as a lone poet limping at the heels of his
renowned precursors. Here he sees that "in one pulse the actor
died." He laments for "the dead of a long-dead nation" (a Roman
or British heyday, perhaps, or some realm of his imagination).
His attitude is ambivalent. "The ulcer burst beneath the ointment" of his illusions, so now, "hunched by a sky drawn close,"
all his masks fallen away, he is seen in his true aspect, the
lonely old man, the solitary wanderer who must tread a road
of "weary gravel." He longs for a return of "the grease-paint
and the mask" as ointment for his "mortal sickness," but realizes
that they will not serve. Partly adopted, the solitary role is forced
upon him by his own mortality. He has chosen it as an artist.
He is compelled to it as a human being. His human situation
is defined circumstantially by environment. The interaction of
these factors is the point at which appearance and reality meet.

At one moment in the *Notebooks of Malte Laurids Brigge,*
Rilke has Malte write:

" . . . . I wished the window had been barricaded, blocked up,
like the wall. For now I knew that things were going on out there
in the same indifferent way, that out there, too, there was nothing
but my loneliness." [11]

Mason's sense of the universe and of himself in it, and his sense
of himself in New Zealand, which he had once written of as
a "fools's paradise," come together at the point where he realizes
his own "loneliness" as artist. Probably the dead weight of his
feeling about his own mortality is a primary element in creating
the strong sense of isolation we find in his work. His actual
circumstances, of being what he himself called "a minor artist"
in a tiny, remote and circumscribed society, whose values were
practically those of the English lower-middle class, must have
reinforced his feeling of being an inconsiderable and fated creature in a universe beyond our comprehension.

CHAPTER EIGHT

Balm for Flesh

Sex as a Theme

GLOOMY, sexy and sardonic . . . !"—according to more
than one critic a harsh sexuality is a leading characteristic of Mason's poetry. If we put aside the "Sonnet to Mac-
Arthur's Eyes" and "Tria Carmina ad Miram," the latter published as recently as Mason's Dunedin years (but apparently
first written a good many years earlier), his career as poet is
enclosed by "Sonnets at the Ocean's Base"[1] at one end and
"Flow at Full Moon" at the other. Each of these poems is related to a return to source ("back to the womb"). They are
vastly different in effect. The protagonist of the sonnets regards
his submarine experience as a kind of death, an imprisonment
or captivity from which he must escape. The sequence culminates in escape and this may be interpreted in terms of re-birth.
Flowing beautifully, evoking the experience of a return to
source, "Flow at Full Moon" carries an hypnotic undertone of
completion, acceptance, resignation, a suggestion of willing,
willed annihilation. Either poem may, one supposes, be claimed
as having sexual relevance. Otherwise, as far as the early work
is concerned, we would be hard put to it to discover sexual
references or even any covert sexual theme. The single plain
exception is "Fragment," in *Penny Broadsheet* (*CP*, p. 47) where
the anecdote of the "adulterous pair" is used simply to illustrate
the generalization that:

> hot love will dare
> all things for love's sake everywhere.

William Plomer, who established the critical view of Mason as a "sexy" writer, gives no evidence of having seen any of his work other than the single volume *No New Thing*, the only book in which "the sex theme" is prominent. About one third of the twenty-five poems are overtly concerned with sex, but it is in keeping with the generally centripetal nature of Mason's world that he is largely involved with the *idea* of sex. As we have seen in Chapter V, several times Mason counterbalances mortality with sexual fulfilment. In only one poem, "The Young Man Thinks of Sons" (*CP*, p. 60), does he consider the possible material outcome of "the lust of my loins." This is the poem's central impulse, a Horatian denial of the value, even the moral rightness, of propagation. Mason's hunger for immortality gives it its peculiar tension. We know from other poems ("Sonnet of My Everlasting Hand" is an instance) of his intense interest in processes of generation, evolution, continuation. Here all this is denied, over-ridden by his tremendous sense of human mortality.

From one point of view we may cite the poem as evidence of his intense preoccupation with sex at that period. Its archetypal images—ship, sword, plough—are obviously sexual.[2] "The ship of doom" is life itself, commitment, and the treatment of these images (with that of the pen using not one drop of its ink) is life-denying. A celebration of human life and a simple longing to continue, to live on timelessly—if these are the mainsprings of Mason's psyche, is it not a paradox that he should reject fatherhood? Would it not, at least, be a kind of completion? For many, procreation and parenthood are an assurance of immortality. Here, instinctively, Mason arrived at Unamuno's conclusion that to invest one's life entirely in one's children is "a sterile sacrifice by which nobody profits" and that

It is inhuman . . . to sacrifice one generation of men to the generation which follows, without having any feeling for the destiny of those who are sacrificed without having any regard, not for their memory, not for their names, but for them themselves.

All this talk of a man surviving in his children or in his works, or in the universal consciousness, is but vague verbiage, which satisfies only those who suffer from affective stupidity . . . [3]

It is probably by design that "The Young Man Thinks of Sons" is placed where it is in *No New Thing*. The poems immediately following are all either directly sexual or have sexual overtones. Allen Curnow, who finds the influence of D.H. Lawrence "apparent enough" in such poems, is not alone in holding that view. Yet, while poems such as "Flattering Unction" (*CP*, p. 61), "Lugete O Veneres" (*CP*, p. 62) and "Ad Mariam" (*CP*, p. 112) are charged with some degree of Lawrence's violence, the resemblance is otherwise superficial. Lawrence's purposeful treatment of sex is far removed from Mason's. In Mason's sex poems there is a high degree of onanism. The harshest, including those mentioned immediately above, are quite alien to the compassion of, say, "On the Swag."

Onanism

"Flattering Unction" and "Lugete O Veneres" are onanistic poems in spite of the other figures called up in them. In the first the situation is speculated, the conclusion generalized. What strength the poem has derives from the Catullian vividness of the opening. "Lugete O Veneres," a parody (or something akin to a parody) of a specific poem of Catullus's, is as directly onanist as some of the chants in Whitman's "Song of Myself." The inward-turning which drives Mason to celebrate life and deplore death here, in a debased form, drives him into an attitude of self-love somewhat redeemed by a tinge of satire. Its onanistic drive can hardly be described as "sexy" in any full or positive sense.

These two are the most anguished of a grouping of poems which are little more than evocations or crude expressions of physical frustration. Yet each, to one degree or another, suggests one of Mason's real strengths as a poet, his instinctive method of building a poem dramatically however abstract its initial situation. So often his poems are dramas with one actor, set in a world of isolation and loneliness quite in keeping with the harsh reality of New Zealand in the 'twenties and 'thirties. Even the beautiful "Be Swift O Sun," to the degree that it can be read as a love-poem, is (particularly in its first half) centered upon the lover rather than the beloved. In "She who Steals" (*CP*, p. 63) later in the same book, a woman is described as "the thief of my strength" (i.e. through the sexual act):

> The spirit that burnt up so clearly has all gone out from me:
>   she has stolen my life:
> and I thought like a fool that it was I who won and not she
>   as we lay here at strife.
>
> Now far up on the grey naked mountainside in the great stone's
>   shadow
>   here I sprawl at length
> while ant-like in distance and almost down to the meadow
>   strides the thief of my strength.

This too is, in effect, onanistic. The woman is seen "ant-like in the distance." No suggestion is actually made that there has been bodily commerce between woman and poet. What gives the poem its force, vividness and validity is this sense of the distance between them, the separateness which might never have been otherwise.

Sex as Fulfillment

The nearest Mason comes to a Lawrentian statement is in "The Just Statesman Dies" (*CP*, pp. 72-73) where he has removed the burden of the poem from subjective—I to *persona*. Sexual love is seen by the Just Statesman as life's truest possible fulfillment. Here the Yeatsian conclusion is reached that all the statesman's political and cultural activities are pointless compared with his sexual fulfillment in loving a girl. This alone has made his life complete. Presumably the poem is intended to proclaim the life of instinct over the artificialities of taking thought. Conventional as it is, anyway, the attitude remains merely an idea. Yet, and oddly, the sexual act is evoked through a Christian analogy. Mention of the Feast of Crucifixion, the

>   hands that held me
> far up towards the skies

and his feeling

    like a god
with spirit transcended

may impress as a deeply sexual response, but here, as in the
other "sex" poems, something else is implied. With Mason one
receives not the impression of a fully developed and realized
sex life, but of his idea that this is the epitome of human
experience, at the opposite pole to mortality. Here the sense of
momentary oblivion which is sexually achieved may be com-
plexly related to death's endless oblivion. It may even be an
attempt to replace the permanence with something more con-
trollable, or something which can be regulated.

Woman Rejected

Yet this whole complex of poems has an air of inverted puritanism, a strange quality of self-abasement, even self-punishment.
Closely related to them, at this stage, is the theme of domina-
tion by or rejection of the mother-figure, upon which is built
one of his finest pieces, "Footnote to John II: iv":

Don't throw your arms around me in that way:
    I know that what you tell me is the truth—
    yes I suppose I loved you in my youth
    as boys do love their mothers, so they say,
    but all that's gone from me this many a day:
    I am a merciless cactus an uncouth
    wild goat a jagged old spear the grim tooth
    of a lone crag. . . . Woman I cannot stay.

Each one of us must do his work of doom
    and I shall do it even in despite
    of her who brought me in pain from her womb,
    whose blood made me, who used to bring the light
    and sit on the bed up in my little room
    and tell me stories and tuck me up at night.

Scornful in tone, the epigraph ("Woman, what I have to do
with thee?") well fits the poem.

The dramatic son-mother conflict here hardly needs pointing out. Willed rejection of the mother is the initial dramatic impulse, but the inward process of rejection is not complete. There are ironic reverberations in tone which run counter to the statement, a certain bravado in the last four lines of the octet, a gathering momentum which conveys some kind of inner hysteria. After the abrupt return to reality which concludes the octet, the sestet sounds like an explanation, a rationalization and this modulates in the second half into softening memories, a diminuendo which endows the poem with its peculiar poignancy and yet has also the air of second thoughts beginning to crowd in. Beyond directly personal implications, this may be read as casting aside a particular phase of or attitude to life, as a rejection of Christianity even, or of the European past, "the mother country."

Fairburn's moving "Rhyme of the Dead Self" makes an interesting comparison:

> Tonight I have taken all that I was
> and strangled him that pale lily-white lad . . .

The deft, externalized conclusion:

> he is dead pale youth and he shall not rise
> on the Third day or any other day
> strangled like a snakeskin there he lies
> and shall not trouble me again for aye.[4]

By implication, Fairburn totally rejects his "romantic" youth and also the myth of Christianity. His poem has not the depth of the Mason, but although it is obviously a personal statement about his own life, he achieves a detachment not available to Mason. The Mason sonnet is unusual in that it begins with a climax. A vehemence in the opening suggests that he has had to force himself to offer the rejection. He has none of Fairburn's confidence and, though greatly needing to slough off an old habit of life and thought, at the last he cannot but look back wistfully upon the "infinite riches" of his "little room." While the last lines of the octet are full of aggressively masculine

sexual images, they cease abruptly, cut off short by the protagonist's need to blurt out his intention of cutting away, and
when they cease he turns back for confort to childhood
memories. Coming at that point, the sestet's second line reads
like a childish boast. With the richness of potential meanings
behind the phrases, "tell me stories" and the double sense of
protection and captivity in "tuck me up at night," the final line
is charged with a multiple irony.

Where we get the verbal illusion that "She Who Steals," for
example, is necessarily a poem of deflation expressing reactions
to the completed sex act, there are several urgent poems whose
theme (again related to Catullus) is to press for sexual fulfillment because this is the fullest affirmation of life, after which
is only the void of death:

> Thigh to thigh and lip to lip
> in the long grass we lie
> the cup brims high but we dare not sip
>
> Girls don't think that we were meant
> to take it and drink
> to blend and sink back in drowsed content?
>
> But the seconds pass the moment's gone
> and the rustling grass
> breathes a dead mass and an orison
>
> And two night birds toll from a star-lit bough
> dirge-voiced the waves roll
> as though a soul were passing now.

One such poem, "If it be not God's law" (*CP*, p. 67) carries
Mason's often-reiterated curse upon priests and asserts that he
will suffer damnation willingly to achieve the desired conjunc-
tion. It is a gesture here, no more, although the conclusion
includes a note of apparently social irony:

> to you I'll pour such a libation
> as shall bring me to share your damnation
> when the chosen of God discover.

Conjectural posthumous fame, toil and honour are foresworn in "Since flesh is soon" (*CP*, p. 68) for

> Is not all I was made for
>   bright on her lips?
> does not my whole purpose
>   glow from her hips?
>
> Should not my whole right be
>   to kiss her eyes?
> is not all good
>   held in her thighs?

The two stanzas are formulated as a series of questions. No answers are given, for this is another poem before the fact.

Summation of all these poems is in "Nox Perpetua Dormienda" (*CP*, p. 69), whose title is taken from Catullus's line, "Nox est perpetua una dormienda" and whose theme is Catullian. The Roman, however, was much more vitally sensual. "Vivamus, Mea Lesbia" was, in him, a true strong note despite his sardonic realization that, love whom we may and deeply as we may, death will bring our love to an end. Mason here makes much more of the death, the beauty and the death in complete conflict. Picturing the girl, whose eyes are "dark like a deep black pool in the night," dead, transmogrified to fleshless green bone deep in the wet earth, he concludes, again, on that haunting question:

> What will it help us then girl not to have loved,
>   chill and exposed to the rain or cramped and
>   deep-sodden
> wet to the bone of a truth and mute and unmoved
> then whom will it help that we loved not when we
>   were bodied?

In the ensuing poem (*CP*, p. 70) a more generalized piece, love is depicted as a "grim citadel" strongly built to withstand any onslaught, but time continues on its relentless course,

> and Chaos bids ten thousand years
> run to erase our straw-built folly.

Women in Recent Poems

If we look for a common element in the group in *Recent Poems* we find that each of the five poems is centred upon a woman or an attitude to a woman. These poems also have a most odd effect in their juxtaposition. "Flow at Full Moon," placed last, is (together with "On the Swag" and "Judas Iscariot") one of Mason's most integrated poems. Each of the other four shows symptoms of disintegration. Vivid reality alternates with grossest melodrama, strained language combines with beautifully controlled rhythms, cruelty offset by sentimentality. Of these, "Vengeance of Venus" (*CP*, p. 89) is a curious piece, a mixture of characteristic power and muddled thinking. A somewhat Lolita-like Venus is recalled

> as in Paphos of old
> when your purple swans came trailing
> a white chariot beneath skies of gold.

Venus's laws are broken, apparently, for a vague figure with "French blood and green-brown eyes" (Perhaps the same figure as in "Be Swift O Sun"?). The strained effect, uncertainty of tone, may be indicated by the heavy-handed reference to Christ in stanza six ("for Christ's sake, put down that whip"). The real point and power, however, comes in the last three stanzas (6-9), with a half-ironical attitude to Venus's world and influence brought out in the final stanza:

> The arrogant is humble
> and the fierce old wild-cat is tame:
> just drop that goad and I'll shamble
> once again through your damned hoops
> of shame.

One poem in the Uncollected section of *CP* (p. 110), "Lullaby and Neck Verse," shares with "Departure" (*CP*, p. 91) in connecting a woman-figure and a Housmanish preoccupation with execution. Here Mason gains a powerful effect by the same method as in his "Body of John" poem, alternating juxtaposition.

Four lines of lullaby are interwoven with four lines, oracular in their brevity, obliquely suggesting that the infant of the lullaby has become the unkempt condemned man. Many reverberations are set up by the contrast. We learn nothing about the condemned man, but the references to Calvary and to the mother-figure make him seem a Christ-like figure:

> Oh snuggle down, my baby, your cheek is soft and warm
> *A stubble beard unkempt*
> And sleep you now soundly safe on your mother's arm
> *Wild oats have threshed out hemp*
>
> Ah nestle down safe on your loving mother's knee
> *There is not any hope*
> While Jesus watches over you, who died on Calvary
> *A lank snake of a rope.*

The line,

> *Wild oats have threshed out hemp*

connects the criminal's imminent fate with his breaking away from the mother, his "sowing his wild oats."

Everywhere in Mason's work we find two distinct ideas of women, two responses to them. On the one hand there is the rejected or lost mother and on the other the lover pleaded for, imagined, but never attained. Sometimes there is a suggestion of partial attainment, but this is swiftly followed by retribution (as in "Vengeance of Venus," where the vengeful figure could as well be a mere protector). Apart from the complexities of "Flow at Full Moon," where the mother and lover-figures merge, nowhere there is any true sense of sexual fulfillment. Once or twice spoken of as the only desirable goal of human existence, this could well be because it is a goal never reached. Thus, it is an exaggeration to say, as some critics have, that Mason is sex-preoccupied. He appears to use the sexual life of his imagination when he is seeking a handy summary for all that is most vivid, positive and desirable in human existence.

CHAPTER NINE

Unflinching in the Fiery Van

A LTHOUGH none of it approaches the quality of his best
poetry, no account of Mason's work would be complete
without some consideration of his political writings. Much of
his life has been taken up with political activity, political issues
and political causes.

Early Political Poems

Nicely characterizing Mason's editorship of the two issues
of *Phoenix* for 1933, Curnow tells us that it was accomplished
"with a bravura, a passionate indignation against social wrong
and inequality, and scorn of public stupidities that revealed
the nature of the poet he was, as well as of the pamphleteer
he considered himself."[1] Much earlier we have Curnow's bald
statement in the 1945 edition of the Caxton anthology, "He professes Communism." To describe him as politically very much
of the Left is perhaps accurate enough. This description can
be most easily tested on the journalism, chief record of his
political preoccupations and activities. To a much lesser degree
it is to be discovered also in the poetry, including a few unpublished verses and epigrams, which, of no great merit in
themselves, reveal another facet of Mason's talent.

Among the very earliest work in *CP* we find in "Lullaby"
(*CP*, pp. 19-20) a diatribe against the greedy, tyrannical capitalist who subjugates fellow creatures to "filthed machine-like toil,"
in contrast with a better-known, though less typical, statement
of the same period, the submissiveness incidental to "The Lesser

Stars." A comparable divergence may be discerned between the first and third quatrains of another early poem, "The Agnostic" (*CP*, p. 26), and in the strange dichotomy between the horde and the few elect of a somewhat later poem, "In Manus Tuas Domine" (*CP*, p. 78). Enigmatic, this has the climactic force of a self-induced sexual experience, and also poses the interesting question: Why does Mason choose to place this frenetic evocation of overwhelming hordes at the conclusion of his book? Whenever he employs the image or figure of a horde or mob it is presented unsympathetically, sometimes fearfully (as here). When in later poems he refers to his fellow men hopefully or approvingly he seems mostly to be responding to a collective abstraction.

Not until the mid-'thirties, in *End of Day*, do we find "Youth at the Dance":

> Get your machineguns manned
> for a new way of war:
> can you not understand
> that here is a foe at hand
> you have not fought before.
> Young blood, in the dance
> you are graceful and wellgroomed
> and move with an elegance—
> ah is it not evil chance
> that your blood and grace are doomed.
> Come young blood leave your prattle
> now the machinegun chatters
> and your tamed and trusted cattle
> turn like an old bull to battle
> and rip their lords to tatters:
> The lone hand digging gum
> and the starving bushie outback
> girls from the stews and the slum
> and the factoryhell . . . up they come
> to the tune of the devil's attack,

which is Mason's only poem directly expressing the political passions of the time.[2]

"MacArthur's Eyes"

From then on he became increasingly involved in political and trades union journalism. Some propaganda verse was published in the late 'thirties and early 'forties, but one "political" poem—published in 1950 after a verse silence of nearly a decade—has, perhaps because of the silence, become something of a Mason landmark, the widely-known "Sonnet to MacArthur's Eyes" (*CP*, p. 103). Prompted by the Korean war, this is certainly a propagandist poem, but that is not what is ultimately important about it. All Mason's horror of death wells up again as forcefully and eloquently as of old. His sense of history is balanced against that overwhelming empathy, so characteristic in him, with a moment, or a small object, of beauty. His abhorrence of death is thrown into poignant relief by the image of spring flowers:

> I have known old eyes that had seen many more
> aspects of warfare than this man has seen—
> eyes that had looked on Gallipoli or the keen
> edge of battle with the Boers or in even older war
> had known Balaclava and the Mutiny's evil score:
> such eyes as I've known them old have always been
> eager to see spring flowers and the youth who mean
> mankind's spring after war's winter. Never before

> Have I known of anyone whose old eyes rejoice
> to see young men lying dead in their own land.
>   (*CP*, p. 103)

The climax of his feeling of horror is contained in one word, "quavering,"

> never have I known one who of his own choice
> follows up the machines of death to take his stand
> over the slain and in a quavering voice
> declaim his joy at youth dead beneath his hand.

MacArthur was reported, on seeing the bodies of dead young soldiers, to have said, "That's a good sight for my old eyes."

To the poet it is all but incomprehensible that one who is himself so near death should wish its final horror on the young. Its unquestionable dignity saves the poem from any charge of subjective partiality. Yet finally one must agree with C.K. Stead, that it "is rendered superfluous by MacArthur's remark quoted as its epigraph, the brutality of which declares itself more forcibly than anything the poem can do."[3]

"Prelude," looked at already in relation to Mason's view of the poet's role, was presumably written as a programme poem to introduce *This Dark Will Lighten.* If Mason's palpable horror of death is an inversion of an intense feeling for life, the present affirmation would seem to be taking its natural place at a point where the poet has become more capable of objectivity; but the philosophy of present hope, with its corollary of rejected tradition, is too consciously rationalized. In view of what we know of Mason's general attitude to life at that time, all the expected responses are to be discovered within the poem. Life's checks and limitations are summed up and the blame for them apportioned to "fat priests." The stoical "I have no child of the flesh" is seen as a victory over the priests, and even the poems unwritten are not grudged because of "the scarlet in the sky of the east," which tells us that the day of true celebration is about to arrive, the new awakening. If, as is most often said, he is deeply a pessimist, this would be a superficial reaction to life's problems. Whatever may be his deeper impulses, "Prelude" is not rooted in them. It remains stubbornly the statement of an idea, product of a non-poetic impulse.

Journalism

Mason's active involvement as a political writer first became truly apparent in 1931-32, with a number of articles, letters and reviews in *The New Zealand Worker* and *Farming First.* These include criticism of the pro-German attitudes of the national daily *The New Zealand Herald.*

Straightforward journalistic-political commentary apart, much of his propagandist work in these years is in parable form, for example the anti-capitalist short story, "The Mountain of the

Gods," published in *Tomorrow* in 1935. The brief "plays" (sometimes described as "poems") published at intervals throughout
his career usually have the terseness of parables. Scripts of these
works are no longer available, though perhaps a dozen of them
have been produced, "published" or circulated, mostly in the
period 1938—1950. One, very early, *The Man from Verstche-
ginski* (of which a copy was sighted by the present writer some
years ago) is not listed in Traue's bibliography, but is of incidental interest as a pleasant skit on Communism and its effect on
the inhabitants of an isolated village.

Plays and Mass-Recitations

Mason's earliest published play is the Caxton booklet *Squire
Speaks* (printed in Auckland by the Unicorn Press, printers of
No New Thing, 1938), performed in Auckland in December,
1939, by the People's Theatre, an offshoot of the Workers'
Educational Association. E.H. McCormick's brief judgment, that
the play "reads like a sketchy caricature of Auden and Isher-
wood"[4] is pointed enough to make further comment risk seeming
ponderous. "To Save Democracy," published in *Tomorrow* in
the same year, has more substance than *Squire Speaks,* but it is
too brief to develop into a satisfactory play. It concerns a con-
scientious objector who has been forcibly dragged to the
trenches. Its core is a discussion between one Captain Vincent,
the militaristic, anti-socialist Commanding Officer and Baker,
the badly-mauled objector, a socialist. Two other characters are
sketched, their presence to show the natural goodness and ob-
tuseness of the common soldier. Vincent and Baker each begins
a statement of his point of view, but situation and statement
remain static. The initial irony, that the brutal and warlike
Vincent believes himself the saviour of democracy, is left to
speak for itself and the whole scene is not taken beyond the
level of left-wing stock-response.

From mid-1939 we have the whole series of Mason's contributions to the Communist weekly, *The People's Voice.* First of
these, a poem for two voices written in memory of the International Brigade in Spain, is a paean of praise for the "young

fellows whistling," "free, straight, with wise eyes," in contrast
to the "ruling classes/ignorant, fanatical, merciless." A similar
antithesis is the foundation for a series of brief articles on the
"Spirit of the Pioneers" in early New Zealand. These concern
the lot of the labouring man in the early days of New Zealand's
pakeha history. Factually, they contain material of real interest
within the context, but the attitude from which they are written
is "romantic" in a way which has not worn particularly well.

In September, 1939, *The People's Voice* published Mason's
"The Dark Will Lighten" described as "a poem for mass-recita-
tion. Those who know this form—so common in progressive
theatres abroad—will supply for themselves a scheme of movement, lighting and response of voices." What follows is an evocation of the harsh conditions of the workers, "of our comrades"

> of those who are more than our kindred,
> of those fellow-workers and dear companions

and of old associations in strike action, dull job, committee or
"Marxian class." The whole piece rises somewhat towards poetry
in the final strophe, but it is held back by the overt propagan-
dizing. Similarly-based, "Skull on Silence," is tauter and its open
campaigning gains by being a strong counterblast to "*Dulce et
decorum est pro patria mori.*" Reminiscent of both Whitman and
Sassoon, it suffers because it has been done in just this way
more than once before:

> Come along over
> and live in the land of skulls.
> where silence lasts forever,
> where for all time there is silence.
>
> There is silence here so deep and dead
> that I cannot even feel the sound
> of the recruiting-sergeant barking for war
> nor the bishop booming for war
> nor the politician yelping for war
> nor the businessman praying for war
> nor the general howling for war . . .

First momentarily bemused by the Soviet-German pact, the moment Russia was involved in the war on the Allies' side Mason produced, for the Aid to Russia Committee, his pamphlet *Help Russia or — Help Hitler!* (1941). Clearly-written, factually-based, this is unaffected by the sentimentalism of his more "literary" attempts at propaganda. Many of its views would be untenable today, in the light of a further quarter-century's passing and our much more detailed knowledge of the Soviet Union, but, as expressed, Mason's position is reasonable and based on a sense of the facts. Here we need note only his aims, to combat the widespread lies (a) that "Russia is so badly run she couldn't help us," (b) that "the Red Army is so weak it wouldn't be any good" and (c) that "the Russians never really wanted to co-operate with us."

Much later in the war, in December 1944, his article on "The Churches and the United Front," published in *In Print,* throws a great deal of light on his religious and political views, at least at that time. He speaks of those who have been "emancipated from religion," noting that they are in a small minority every-where. However, he observes, it is quite wrong to suppose that only those who are so "emancipated" are capable of embracing socialism (i.e. Marxism). He pursues his argument by separating Christian "faith" and the Christian ethic:

It is, of course, the supernatural element in religion with which dia-lectical materialism is irreconcilable. Christian ethics—in the 'brother-hood of man' form—are not confined to Christianity; they are part of the common heritage of enlightened mankind with origins running far back beyond the Christian era. Marxists have never attacked those ethics . . .[5]

He concludes by claiming that, anyway, religious believers and non-believers have united in revolutionary struggle and that (particularly as there has been some process of democratization within the churches themselves) "the Labour Movement" should be prepared to co-operate with them in the fight against fascism.

Issued in printed form in 1943 and later produced by Margaret Barr as part of a double-bill, with Mason's *Refugee,* the dance drama *China* is the chief link-point in his work between poetry and politics. Presumably referring to such pieces as "The Dark Will Lighten" and "Skull on Silence," he notes in the preface to *China*:

. . . . It has been my lot at various times to write a fair number of similar plays for special purposes and for production in such places as union and political meetings, street demonstrations . . . even a church.[6]

He claims little knowledge of the actual situation in China. What captures his imagination is "that glorious spirit of resistance to barbarism." Beyond that, what appeals to him is a Marxist picture of dignified co-operative labour:

> One man cannot even stir the log
> that a score can run with.

The drama's concluding dream is of

> none brighter in the world's firmament,
> united and free China,
> all-powerful yet gentle.

A pleasant enough picture, *China* lacks the depth of the best poetry, because there is no discovery in it, simply an illustration of the Marxist ideal.

Refugee[7] is in seven prose scenes, concerned with the question of whether "foreign" refugees ought to be admitted into New Zealand. One of its points is that "Fascist" and "German" are not synonymous, that Fascism is to be found in New Zealand itself, as it may be found everywhere. The war was a war against Fascism. After the opening scene, a debate in which plea is made for admission and acceptance of non-British refugees into the country, the remaining scenes display Mason's habitual preoccupations. Scene Two is largely mime, the coming of the Maori; Scene Three is concerned with Irish refugees; Scene Four portrays the escape of two convicts from the Australian penal colony; in Scene Five three mid-nineteenth-century working-class people are about to set off for a fresh life in New Zealand;

Scene Six deals with homesickness; in Scene Seven, Jewish persecution in pre-1939 Germany merges with the "frame" situation of the public meeting in which the refugees, after all, prove their point. The whole ends in a Chant of Exultation. While it has a certain charm, it is stock material, in situation and dialogue. It tells us something about Mason as a man, but adds nothing to his measure as a writer.

New Zealand's Forsaken Frontier

From at least 1931, when he wrote articles on Samoa and the missionaries, his interest in the lot of the Pacific Islanders is evident. At the moment when *China* was published he contributed a piece to *The People's Voice*, "Pacific Islands Need Atlantic Charter,"[8] pointing the contrast between the Hollywood version and the actualities of disease, drugs, slave-labour and the breaking down of native institutions. A few months later, in *In Print*, we find him commenting approvingly on the Australia—New Zealand agreement on Native Peoples of the Pacific.[9]

This concern with the Pacific Islands led to his most extended piece of political writing, *Frontier Forsaken*, published by Challenge in 1947. Described as "An Outline History of the Cook Islands," this essay is not history in any scholarly or academic sense. It is polemic, clearly-written journalism with a definite aim—the improvement in political and social condition of the Cook Island natives. Only in 1965 did the Cook Islanders achieve independence with a genuine promise of help in bettering the appalling conditions of life in the Territories. Their situation twenty years ago would quite naturally have aroused the revolutionary in Mason, the more so as they are Maoris closely akin to the Maoris of New Zealand.

Describing his work as "the first printed history and general survey of the Cook Islands" (*FF*, p. 5), he opens the account with typical rhetoric: "Your gaze has swung over the vast arc of the Pacific Ocean, as it runs almost the full length of the world, with its multitude of islands fanning out . . ." (p. 5). Evidence of a love of rhetoric, Maori, Celtic, Chinese, can be discerned at many points throughout his career and, in his own public readings at their best, he performed with an entirely convincing rhetorical flourish. Here, however, he soon abandons any gestures and gets down to plain dealing.

As Algeria was to metropolitan France so the Cook Islands were regarded, and were established politically, as an integral part of New Zealand. Thus the widely scattered, and greatly differing, islands were New Zealand's northern frontier, the "frontier forsaken." Before New Zealand took control, the Islands had been ruled by Britain. As in a great many other cases in the Pacific and elsewhere, the arrival of Europeans brought disease, exploitation, tyranny and neglect. Mason establishes his ground for discussion and protest:

> Yet they survived, and, when the New Zealand government took over control, they were winning their way back uphill to their rightful place among the peoples of mankind.
> Once again they were driven downhill.
> We found them free and we reduced them to servitude.
> We found them prosperous and we reduced them to direst poverty. (p. 6)

A wide range of tropical fruits could be prepared and exported from the Islands, but mainly to New Zealand. In spite of the fact that this would be of great benefit to Islands and mainland alike this industry has been encouraged only sporadically and developed in the most haphazard fashion.

Briefly sketching the arrival in the various islands of both Polynesian and white man (known, he says, to the Polynesians as "Kookes"), he continues by outlining the melancholy effect of the latter, in spite of the Rarotongans (for example) praying to their gods to send *them* the white man. Whatever the theories, the facts are that:

> . . . for long years over vast areas in the Pacific, Europeans looted, destroyed, slew, incited warfare, kidnapped, enslaved, blackbirded, debauched, corrupted with alcohol and contaminated with disease.

Even when they came with high ideals—as did most missionaries
and some administrators—too often the results of their actions were
unintentionally disastrous, in introducing disease and destroying the
basis of the native social system. (p. 36)

In contrast with the poetry's anti-clericalism, he is quick to
assure us here that the missionaries alone attempted to introduce
beneficial elements of the European type of social system. They
taught writing and developed education generally (teaching,
among the more obvious subjects, agriculture, hygiene, astron-
omy and even "simple trades"—p. 45). Most important of all,
they had recognized the value of the native governmental system, which was quasi-democratic, consisting of a council of
chiefs. Substituting a system of official nominees, the New
Zealand administration effectively abolished the traditional role
of this council, the *Are-korero*.

Throughout the Victorian period the Islands' population was
reduced by disease, its source being recognized by the islanders'
phrase for sickness, "I am shippy." Yet, in spite of this and the
destructive effect of misguided zeal in undermining local customs
in sex, dress, housing, and other matters, from the time when
the British protectorate was officially declared in 1888 every
effort was made towards just government by marrying native
custom to a parliamentarian ideal.

Meanwhile the New Zealand government, was using dis-
gruntled Cook Island *pakehas* as spies to undermine the existing
authorities. At the turn of the century Seddon[10] visited the islands
briefly and, in September 1900, they were formally annexed by
the New Zealand parliament. Later, from the beginning of the
First World War to the end of the Second, comes what Mason
describes as "the period of absolute annihilation of native rights"
(p. 70). The Cook Islands Government Act of 1915 suspended
democratic government. Exploitation ensued of the Cook Islands
fruitgrowers, who found it quite impossible to obtain viable
prices for their produce. In its turn this resulted in a policy
of "indebtedness" or capitalist exploitation whereby growers
could, in the last analysis, be deprived of their estates for debt
by white shippers. Wage earners at the same time were receiving

a pittance which contrasted unfavourably with workers' wages in almost all other Pacific island groups.

During this same period many Cook Island natives were shanghaied and removed into slavery by Peruvian slave-traders. In 1945 a scandal of this kind, "the worst labour scandal in New Zealand history" (p. 81), brought more official interest to the Islands and seemed, for a time, as if it could result in improved conditions. More than four hundred Cook Island natives had been taken away to work in virtual slavery for a French commercial concern and forced to live in filthily insanitary barracks on bread and tea and without medical or recreational arrangements. Through Princess Te Puea the New Zealand Maoris pressed for action as also did the Trades Council on the question of wages. All this occurred at a time when the United Nations Charter was being drafted:

> By this time it should have been clear that the issues involved were greater than a waterside dispute, greater even than general wages and conditions; it was the awakening of a people to achieve unity, control of its own affairs and the right to play its part in the world.
> Precisely at this time New Zealand representatives at international conferences were most clamorous about the rights of small nations. (p. 87)

Socialist as he is, Mason does not here seek to make party political discriminations from the Cook Islands' appalling condition. If he has a villain in mind it is a Labour MP, Arthur Osborne, described in a photograph caption as one "whose superficial investigations and complacent reports must be held very largely responsible for the creation of the rift between the Cook Island people and the Government" (p. 75). On the other hand, he attacks details of an orange-planting scheme of that time, which was accompanied by the surveying of land to be broken up into individual smallholdings in order to create "a landowning class of native Maoris, at the expense of the majority of their kith and kin, who are rendered landless" (p. 96). Finally he shows how the New Zealand mainland Maoris have been much better treated than their Cook Island "elder brothers." In effect, since the Cook Islands were always claimed to be an integral part of the country, the whole of the "forsaken frontier" shows as forthright an example of racial and social discrimination as can be found anywhere.

Brief as it is, this account of Mason's political journalism may serve to widen the context in which his other, more interesting work is set. As writing, the one virtue we can claim for his political material at its best is that of economy. Otherwise, from the *Phoenix* days to *Frontier Forsaken* and the everyday journalism of *Challenge* we observe a man dominated by the Marxist ideal, one for whom humanitarianism and brotherhood come before all else. Sometimes it is said that his increasing absorption in political and social problems finished him as a poet. That is a question impossible to decide. The young poet death-conscious because of his love of this life does, however, seem to be naturally of a piece with the later Mason, advocate of the co-operation and brotherhood of man.

CHAPTER TEN

They Are Gone and I Am Here

W E have ample evidence of classical Latin influence on Mason's work, but other influences were almost as important. Nothing before him in the poetry of his own country could have helped him much. In his "Song of Allegiance" (*CP*, p. 45) he appears to regard himself as a poet in the main stream of the English tradition. He names as his illustrious predecessors Shakespeare, Milton, Keats, Shelley, Byron, Wordsworth, Coleridge, Beddoes, Tennyson and Housman. Several points about this list are notable. There is no mention of Burns, Mason's interest of many years, nor of any Celtic poet (one might have expected Moore, or even Mangan or Davis). It is less surprising that Yeats and Eliot are absent, but Donne's presence is therefore all the more unexpected.

Influences: Humbert Wolfe

In a conversation just before he died, Fairburn insisted that Humbert Wolfe was a large influence on Mason.[1] Wolfe, in that period before the war, was an extraordinarily popular and influential versifier. That there is some truth in Fairburn's suggestion can be borne out by examining Mason's poem "The Seventh Wound Protests" (*CP*, p. 107). Treatment of subject suggests that it could have been written as early as "Oils and Ointments" (1925). Schematically it is very like the carol "The Twelve Days of Christmas." It also strikingly resembles, in method and thought, Humbert Wolfe's "A Chant."[2] Technically and tonally, Mason's work quite often is akin to Wolfe's. Both poets tend to use a markedly short or a markedly long line (as in the present instance). Each makes more than common use of soft line endings. The occasional similarity of tone is matched in choice of subject, but Mason's is the more robust and masculine talent. For all Wolfe's facility, today a large proportion of his work rings false. Thus a comparison of the two poets' work need not be pursued in further detail.

If we look again at Mason's list we find in it a predominance of Romantic poets. More than one critic has noticed the "strong Tennysonian undertow" in his work, but there is no evidence of his ever having been affected by the hard thinking of Keats or Coleridge. His list is interesting beyond the range of his own work. Smithyman has noted "the insidious effect of William Wordsworth"[3] on New Zealand poetry. Later, Smithyman expands this in a paragraph of great interest:

So we have Wordsworth established at the head of the board, supported by Shelley, less apparently by Coleridge and dubiously by Keats who was more the object of respectful study by Reeves and his contemporaries. These are not strictly Victorians; we have however received them in what I can only think is a Victorian fashion. The presence of the greater Victorians is another matter. The Tennysonian element in Mason has been mentioned, with whom also Beddoes is associated—I think this unsound—and with whom Hardy should be associated.[4]

Beddoes

He would argue, I believe, for Hardy as an influence on Mason and there is undoubtedly a kinship, both technical and temperamental. Housman's presence in the "Song of Allegiance" is obviously due to his notable combination of classical scholarship and poetry. Beddoes' name is hardest to account for. Smithyman's most astute observation, that we have reacted to the Romantics "in what I can only think is a Victorian fashion" is particularly applicable to Beddoes, who embodied the peculiarly Victorian version of a Romantic poet. Beddoes (and not Hardy) is specifically named in Mason's list. Quite close parallels may be drawn between the work of the two poets and the connection between Beddoes and Mason is greater in extent than may at first appear.

The well-known opening lines of Mason's "The Spark's Farewell to Its Clay" (see above, ch. IV, p. 62) are related in tone and preoccupation to a seven-line Beddoes fragment, which opens:

> I am bewildered—utterly astray
> Within the doubt-brakes of obscurest Thought
> Whereunto at the last I have been brought
> Thro' all diversity of time and way . . .[5]

Balancing long and short lines, a technique of Mason's in "The Young Man Thinks of Sons," "Lullaby and Neck-Verse" and "Lugete O Veneres,"[6] may be found in Beddoes,[7] but there are even closer correspondences in use of rhythms. In a group of three Beddoes song-poems, "The Ghosts' Moonshine,"[8] the opening quatrain of each poem is rhythmically similar to Mason's "Judas Iscariot":

> It is midnight, my wedded;
> Let us lie under
> The tempest bright, my dreaded,
> In the warm thunder.

Closer still is "Song on the Water,"[9] first stanza of which reads:

> As mad sexton's bell tolling
> For earth's loveliest daughter
> Night's dumbness breaks rolling
> Ghostlily
> So on boat breaks the water
> Witchingly.

Different kinds of correspondence to "Judas Iscariot" may be found in Beddoes' "Songs by the Deaths" II[10] and "The New-Born Star." The second of these is slight, a reference to Judas' character:

> Mark ye now
> The death-intending wrinkles of his brow?
> He is the murderous Judas of the world.[11]

The other is a description of Death, recurring:

> Dance and be merry for Death's a droll fellow.

Mason's lines:

> here in this far-pitched perilous hostile place
> this solitary hard-assaulted spot
> fixed at the friendless outer edge of space,

apart from reminding us, as Smithyman suggests, of Arnold's "Dover Beach" and,

> . . . the vast edges drear
> And naked shingles of the world

also reaches back to an echo in Beddoes' "Alfarabi, the World Maker, A rhapsodical fragment":

> . . . within a space
> Upon the very boundary and brim
> Of the whole universe, the outer edge
> Which seemed almost to end the infinite zone.[12]

Such early Mason poems as "After Death," "The Lesser Stars" and, more faintly, "Sonnets of the Ocean's Base, II"[13] correspond in feeling and attitude to part of Beddoes' "Written in an Album at Clifton: March, 1828":

> For now I hear even such an anxious voice
> Crying in my soul's solitude and bewailing
> That I had never in my childhood known
> The bud of this manifold beauteousness,
> And seen each leaf turn on its tender hinge
> Until the last few parted scarce and held
> Deep in their midst a heaven-reflecting gem:
> For then I might—oh vain and flattering wish!—
> I might have stood, tho last, among friends,
> Where I am now the last among the strangers,
> And not have passed away as now I must
> Into forgetfulness, into the cold . . .[14]

In the third fytte of Beddoes' *The Improvisatore* we encounter
a stock figure:

> Amongst the foul carcasses slowly there went
> A reverend hermit weak and bent,
> Muttering prayers with a tremulous tongue,
> Whilst groans of despair at his deafened ears hung.[15]

We meet him again in Mason's "Sonnets of the Ocean's Base"
(*CP*, pp. 21-22) as the "bent old/eremite bodily prone beneath
the stars" whose "flesh/was mouthed by clammy cold and
hideous things" and who paid adoration amid the "skeletons
of sneering dead."

Another early Beddoes poem, "Lines Written at Geneva;
July 16" [1824] strikes ground covered again by Mason in the
final "Sonnet of the Ocean's Base," "A Doubt" and "The Spark's
Farewell to Its Clay":[16]

> The earth is full of chambers for the dead
> And every soul is quiet in his bed;
> Some who have seen their bodies mould away,
> Antediluvian minds—most happy they,
> Who have no body but the beauteous air,
> No body but their minds. Some wretches are
> Now lying with the last and only bone
> Of their old selves, and that one worn alone
> That ate their heart: some, buried just, behold
> Their weary flesh, like an used mansion, sold
> Unto a stranger and see enter it
> The earthquake winds and waters of the pit.[17]

Similarly, relating somewhat more to Mason's "Sonnet of My
Everlasting Hand" (*CP*, p. 48) are the opening lines of a verse
letter to Brian Waller Procter:

> Today a truant from the odd old bones
> And winds of flesh, which, as tamed rocks and stones
> Piled cavernously make his body's dwelling,
> Have housed man's soul.[18]

Another, "Dirge for Wolfram," may be compared with "Be
Swift O Sun" (*CP*, p. 65). The first of its two nine-line stanzas
closes:

> Lie still and deep,
> Sad soul, until the sea-wave washes
> The rim o' th' sun tomorrow,
> In eastern sky.[19]

The conclusion tells of Wolfram's meeting his loved one in
death,

> And then alone, amid the beaming
> of love's stars, thou'lt meet her
> In eastern sky.

Death, who "is more 'a jest' than Life" is described later in
the letter to Procter, mentioned above, in much the same terms
as Mason's Herostratus describes himself. Death can be mocked
only in Epicurean terms, Beddoes believes (the same feeling
is made explicit in Mason's "Nox Perpetua Dormienda" [*CP*,
p. 69], and elsewhere):

> . . . he who fills the cup and makes the jest
> Pipes to the dancers, is the fool o' the feast.
> Who's he? I've dug him up and decked him trim
> And made a mock, a fool, a slave of him
> Who was the planet's tyrant: dotard Death:
> Man's hate and dread: not with a stoical breath
> To meet him like Augustus standing up,
> Nor with grave saws to season the cold cup
> Like the philosopher, nor yet to hail
> His coming with a verse or jesting tale
> As Adrian did and More: but of his night,
> His moony ghostliness and silent might
> To rob him, to uncypress him i' the light
> To unmask all his secrets; make him play
> Momus o'er wine by torchlight is the way
> To conquer him and kill; and from the day
> Spurned, hissed and hooted send him back again
> An unmask'd braggart to his bankrupt den.[20]

The prayer in Beddoes' "Pygmalion" centres upon a situation not far removed from that of "Arius Prays" (*CP,* p. 108). Pygmalion has asked Aphrodite to breathe life into the statue of a woman which he has made and has fallen in love with. This statue is, in a remote way, analogous to Christ, God made man. In Mason's poem Arius prays that Christ remain a man in order to understand man's tragic sense of life. Pygmalion prays that he, as creator and created thing, be saved from death:

> Goddess that made me, save thy son and save
> The man that made thee, goddess, from the grave.
> Thou know'st it not; it is a fearful coop
> Dark, cold, and horrible—a blinded loop
> In Pluto's madhouse green and wormy wall.
> O save me from 't; let me not die, like all,
> For I am but like one—not yet, not yet,
> At least not yet—and why? my eyes are wet
> With the thick dregs of immature despair,
> With bitter blood out of my empty heart,
> I breathe not aught but my own sighs for air,
> And my life's strongest is a dying start.[21]

Among Mason's published poems, the humour of "Latter-Day Geography Lesson" (*CP,* p. 40) is unusual. The concluding lines have a hint of the grisly, common in Beddoes. Mason manages it with a lighter touch:

>   and the Abbey
> lies here under our feet *you great babby*
> *Swift-and-short do-please-kindly-stop-poking*
> *your thumbs through the eyes of that skull.*

Beddoes mentions "the Abbey" ("the sour archbooby who shut Byron/Out of the Abbey") in a fragment in his "Last Poems,"[22] but an earlier piece is an extended example of the sort of order given to "Swift-and-short":

> Thread the nerves through the night holes,
> Get out of my bones, you wormy souls,

> Shut up my stomach, the ribs are full:
> Muscles be steady and ready to pull.
> Heart and artery merrily shake
> And eyelid go up, for we're going to wake—
> His eye must be brighter—one more rub!
> And pull up the nostrils! his nose was snub.[23]

The central concerns of Mason's poetry may be found in the
two parts of "The Spark's Farewell to Its Clay" (*CP*, p. 38), and
here there are several connections with Beddoes and at least
one close parallel. First there is Beddoes' fragment, "Dream
of Dying," which begins,

> Shivering in fever, weak, and parched to sand,
> My ears, those entrances of word-dressed thoughts,
> My pictured eyes, and my assuring touch,
> Fell from me, and my body turned me forth
> From its beloved abode: then I was dead;
> And in my grave beside my corpse I sat,
> In vain attempting to return.[24]

These are complementary to the "Lines written at Geneva"
quoted above, and their relevance to "The Spark's Farewell"
is self-evident. A Beddoes sonnet, the second of a pair called
"A Clock Striking at Midnight"[25] contains hints of "Sonnets of
the Ocean's Base," lines that might well have been written by
Mason himself (e.g. "dragged along to dark destruction's brink").
Most strikingly, however, the ideas in this sonnet correspond
closely with those in both parts of "The Spark's Farewell." Preoccupation with death, Fame (immortality), separation of body
and soul are common to both poets. A noticeable resemblance
between Mason's language and imagery and Beddoes' is never
more evident than here. Linked with the first, this sonnet begins
in mid-sentence,

> And puffs death's cloud upon us. It is vain
>   To struggle with the tide; we all must sink
> Still grasping the thin air, with frantic pain
>   Grappling with Fame to buoy us. Can we think

> Eternity, by whom swift Time is slain,
>   And dragged along to dark destruction's brink,
> Shall be the echo of man's puny words?
>   Or that on grovelling thoughts shall e'er be writ
> In never-fading stars; or like proud birds
>   Undazzled in their cloud-built eyrie sit
> Clutching the lightning, or in darking herds
>   Diving amid the sea's vast treasury flit
>   Sink, painted clay, back to thy parent earth
>   While the glad spirit seeks a brighter birth.[26]

The comparison is complete when we put together Beddoes' closing couplet and the sestet of "Spark's Farewell to Its Clay" II. See page 72.

We find, then, a kindred tone and a preoccupation with death in Mason and Beddoes. Correspondences of language (e.g. in the recurring use, by both poets, of "grovelling," "writ," "eyeball"), of syntax and punctuation. Interestingly, affinities of tone and attitude may be recognized also between Beddoes and Housman. We need not expatiate here, but links are most immediately evident if we compare *The Shropshire Lad* with the Songs from Beddoes' *Outidana*.[27] One example will suffice—the opening of the first song from *The Second Brother*:

> Strew not earth with empty stars,
>   Strew it not with roses,
> Nor feathers from the crest of Mars,
>   Nor summer's idle posies.[28]

Beddoes was not particularly an influence for good on Mason. What, is attributable to Beddoes' influence is a certain strain, the strain which led Roger Savage to characterize Mason's as "a violent poetry." The two poets are also notably introverted and self-preoccupied, though this in Mason cannot be ascribed to any effect Beddoes may have had. In general, Mason's handling of his own melancholy inward-turning is superior to the Victorian poet's because, behind it, there is a positive feeling for life itself.

Housman

We may say that Mason found Beddoes for himself because
he had no forebears in New Zealand poetry to whom he could
turn as sources of strength or emulation. Housman's influence
on Mason is more commonly recognized. Both were informed
by the study of Latin poetry. Similarities between Mason's work
and Housman's are not a matter of exact correspondences, but
of tonal qualities, use of language and a general use of imagery
and "symbol" deriving from similar psychological preoccupations.
The important source for comparison is *A Shropshire Lad*
(1896), since *Last Poems* came too late to affect Mason's work.

In Housman's typical attack, "Now of my threescore years
and ten . . .," consciousness of death, mutability, the sense
of impermanence, all are as they occur in Mason.

There are instructive differences. Housman has a metrical
facility, a smoothness which Mason lacks. Their adroit neat-
ness is the quality which makes many of Housman's poems
memorable. Those few of Mason's poem which have this same
memorableness owe it to other qualities. From a nature less
sophisticated, though possibly deeper, his poems have a heavier
touch, but the same inevitability.

A major difference between them is that Housman is always
at a safe remove from the experience of death. Either he speaks
as the one dead, safely through the trauma of dying (so to
speak), in poems such as "Is My Team Ploughing?"[29] or he
offers encouragement to some other figure who is moving
towards death (his soldiers, for example), or he expects to die,
but he is a youth and death is a long way ahead. Facing the
problem more starkly and squarely, Mason has his protagonist
always, in one way or another, solitary, with few distractions
from death-knowledge.

Both poets present death as last act in a tragic drama, but
Mason's dramas almost always have the focus narrowed to a
single character, with no such alleviants as, "And chiefly I
remember/How Dick would hate the cold." While they may be
cited as reducing weaknesses, Mason's introspection and self-
absorption, and the empty stage they create, allow his protag-

onist to concentrate on his situation with greater intensity and poignancy.

It would be unlike Mason to observe such merely visual loveliness as "the cherry hung with snow" in Housman's "Loveliest of trees the cherry now."[30] Mason's "After Death" is comparable, but it is more "classical," the losses detailed are more generalised. Where Housman genuinely delights in the cherry blossom, the sun "on horses sleek hides" etc. are important to Mason largely because they represent non-death or anti-death. Here is something of a paradox. Housman's poems are fused by nostalgia. To contrast "Is My Team Ploughing" with "After Death" is to discover that Housman reminisces, while Mason's protagonist is in the living present, consumed in spirit by death's inevitability. For him a condition of present life is, near the forefront of his consciousness, a foreboding of death.

Rhythmically, in poems such as "Reveille,"[31] Housman contrives a jauntiness foreign to Mason. Here and elsewhere we find an exhortation to action, which is quite out of keeping with Mason's work. On the other hand:

> Clay lies still . . .
> Breath's a ware that will not keep,

has Mason's tone. This use of "clay," with its overtone suggesting that the living body is as good as dead, is common to both poets. The use of "ware" and the word order of that line achieve a syllabic economy like that to be discovered everywhere in Mason's better poems.

For both men the poignancy of existence is in "the hours/That never are told again," in regret at life's passing away. Housman's manifestation of this often seems the more sentimental. Thus Mason's sardonic, Roman playing off of sensuality and mortality, most fully and directly evoked in "Nox Perpetua Dormienda," corresponds to Housman's,

> And man and maid had best be glad
> Before the world is old,[32]

which is a more muted, more conventional response. Yet a sexual
element permeates Housman's verse, and is indeed one of its
dominant characteristics (again we may recollect all those young
redcoats going out to die), but its note is much less direct
than is Mason's in *No New Thing*.

Mason seldom brings off, or even attempts, Housman's commonly achieved irony (a typical example, "Oh, see how thick
the goldcup flowers," mentioned above). Sure and dexterous,
Housman's line has an epigrammatic quality not found Mason,
but for a rare exception such as "A Doubt" (*CP*, p. 49).

That love for the visible world, which is the very texture
of Housman's poetry, sparks in Mason's only fitfully. What
Mason would celebrate and what he mourns for is himself,
that feeling for his own being of which Unamuno speaks. It is
equally true for him as it is for Housman that the "eye beholds
the heart's desire," but he appears to care little for the particular
scene of the sun burning on the half-mown hill or the music
of the blackbird in the coppice. Such specific visual or aural
experiences can be the *cause* of a Housman poem. For Mason
it is unlikely to be more than an accidental detail in the setting
(usually a dramatic one), as when the swagman is to be brought
into the warmth from "the grey level sleet," or the lover's remoteness is expressed quasi-symbolically by depicting her as "far
up on the grey naked mountainside."

Death by hanging was of peculiar fascination to both poets,
as comparison of Mason's "Their Sacrifice" (used in his playscript *This Bird May Swing*) with poems ix and xvii of
A Shropshire Lad will show. Each tends to use the same
components, noose, crowd, church clock chiming away the
hours. While Housman is always measuring time, Mason rarely
does so. Yet it hardly needs saying that he is conscious of its
major effect, i.e. death. Never sentimental about the incidents
of time, he is acutely aware of its flow. Focal point of this
aspect of his poetry comes at the end of *No New Thing*. "In
Manus Tuas Domine" is a cumulative plea. Generations and
centuries are brought forward, their endeavour and achievement set up as reason for death to be mitigated.

If Mason's response to the world is usually more generalized,

Housman is the more passive. Compare, for example, the conditional mood of Housman's "On your midnight pallet lying"[33] with the positive, if frustrated, suffering of Mason's harshly ironical "Lugete O Veneres,"—or compare the observer in "When I watch the living meet"[34] with "the old vagrant" in Mason's "Flattering Unction" (*CP*, p. 61).

A cursory examination of *A Shropshire Lad* will serve to show that Housman is a master in alternating masculine and feminine rhymes or line-endings, a device employed by Mason in "Stoic Overthrow" (*CP*, p. 77), "Nox Perpetua Dormienda" (*CP*, p. 69) and elsewhere. Rhetorically an important effect in establishing tone, this is useful in creating an air of melancholy, reminiscence, or nostalgia. The two soft beats separated by a line-end pause may give added force to the first long beat of the second line (which is usually an important verb or, sometimes, noun):

> Let us laugh with the dying
> and *smile* upon the slain.[35]

Such a technical device is more flexible than may at first appear. Its effect can be cumulative or antithetical.

Generally speaking, Mason was not a conscious craftsman capable of the alliterative transpositions of ". . . list the bugle/ that blows in lands . . ."; but where he lacks the epigrammatic sharpness which can be produced through antithesis, he is never quite as overtly susceptible as Housman to the charge of melopoeic superficiality. Thus, a further technical distinction between them is that, while Housman gains effects by establishing and maintaining a rhythmical complex, Mason does rather the opposite. The two stanzas of Housman's "Into my heart and air that kills"[36] duplicate each other exactly in rhythm, while the effect of finality is clinched in the second stanza simply by use of shorter vowels and harder consonants. Mason, on the other hand, establishes a ground pattern and gains many effects in his departures from it, as in "Flow at Full Moon." Musically not as strong, Mason is not a vulnerable to the difficulties engendered by employing strongly repetitive sound patterns.

There is obvious kinship between Housman and Mason, mainly shown in correspondences of mood, tone and attitude. Much of Humbert Wolfe's work, in conception and manner, is like inferior Housman. Where Housman and Mason draw the essentials from a small range of archetypal situations and make them live, Wolfe tackles things in much the same way only to reveal insincerity and banality.

CHAPTER ELEVEN

Maker or Medium

T WO questions related to the making of Mason's poetry will now concern us. Each is implied by the larger question which has been the main subject of this book: what kind of a writer was R.A.K. Mason and, in particular, what kind of a poet? First of these subsidiary questions is, can we trace any significant technical development in Mason's poetry during the course of his career? Second: what was his attitude to his role as poet and how, if at all, did this change or develop in the course of the years?

Technical Development

From the beginning, any investigator of his technical development will be confronted by puzzles. One of the earliest poems, the second of the three "Sonnets of the Ocean's Base," remained unpublished (apart from its one appearance in *In the Manner of Men*) for nearly forty years. Presumably this is because he and others recognized the unsatisfactoriness of its pseudo-Romantic jargon and of the archaism which he later pruned out of his poetry generally. Yet his version of "O Fons Bandusiae," written, as has been noted earlier, while he was still a secondary school pupil, has (in spite of archaisms) a remarkable strength and economy:

> HORACE III. XIII
> O fair Bandusian fountain
>   which clearer art than glass
>   to thee I shall account on

the next day that may pass:
to thee I shall devote then
as sacrifice a goat then
which dreams in vain love-battles:
    whose forehead is just curving
with young rough horns such I shall
    give to thee who art deserving
of unmixed wine flowers for
    decoration serving
o fount Bandusian that's what I shall do

The offspring of the wanton
gambolling flock your flood
so ice-cool shall be painting
all with his bright red blood:
of this I shall be donor
to glorify and honour
thee who for wandering flocks
    a pleasant draught affordest
and for work-weary oxen
    a welcome cool accordest
o'er whom in blazing hour
    the dog-star hot no lord is
ho fount Bandusian that's what I shall do

You shall become most famous
    whenas I sing—
a fount which all men name as
a very splendid thing—
whenas I sing the ilex
set all among the silex
the hollow craggy silex:
    then too I shall gabble
of sources where thy waters spring
    far from noise of rabble
and all day in the sparkling sun
    to self alone do baddle
yea fount Bandusian that's what I shall do.

More than once it has been observed that his work is curiously arbitrary, a mixture of strength and banality. In diction he combines the colloquial and the conventional. Yet he cannot be too readily dismissed as a poet whose successes are due entirely to chance. In the earliest poems, those of *In the Manner of Men* and those placed early in *The Beggar,* there are obvious moments of clumsiness and stock response. Yet there is, for example, a distinctive use of hard consonants together with the employment of hard images, of jewelry, stone, adamant, steel. Already, at that stage, however conventional the general conception of meter and rhythm may be, effective use is made of the device of balancing long lines against short. At the same time one of his favourite consonantal sounds, the "l," is used purposively in "The Vigil," where it helps to achieve the poem's dirge-like quality. Sometimes in *The Beggar* a poem ends on a minor note which may convey an impression that Mason is uncertain of his *tone* or his *intention,* or both. "Old Memories of Earth" (*CP*, p. 28) is a case in point, where the conclusion, apparently lacking in incisiveness, somehow remains in the mind. Quoting the concluding eight lines,

> And I am positive that yesterday
>   walking past One Tree Hill and quite alone
>   to me there came a fellow I have known
>   in some old times, but when I cannot say:
>
> Though we must have been great friends, I and he,
>   otherwise I should not remember him
>   for everything of the old life seems dim
>   as last year's deeds recalled by friends to me.

"One wonders," says C.K. Stead, "why these lines, even in their inconsequential tailing off, are so powerful."[1] His answer is that the power comes from sheer sincerity and naked honesty and yet, as we shall see (and have seen in relating Mason's work with Housman's), Mason as a craftsman was not without guile. Similar modulations are observable in "The Vigil" and "In Perpetuum Vale," partly explained in the latter case by the poem's curtailment after its first publication in *The Beggar.*[2] Command typical of this early period may be demonstrated by "The Lesser Stars" (*CP*, p. 30), a poem of considerable power, in which life is extracted from a set of fairly conventional images. Its emotional charge derives partly from the management of alternating line lengths, and partly from the grouping of images, all of brevity, transience. The quick pace of the long lines is established syllabically and contrasted (again syllabically) with the deliberateness of the short ones. Hemus has compared this poem, technically, with its Latin source, Horace's Ode III/30.

Horace's poem hums and booms like a great monument itself, with its mighty play on "m" and "n" sounds. Mason's poem gains something of the same effect with its brilliant use of rhyme-play on long-drawn vowels: "outlast brass," "pass," "grass," "alas," beautifully modulating into "alas alas for his too-swift passing away;" "thought," "out," "short," "wrought," "cloud-caught," and so on. Mason's use of short lines also has something of Horace's technique in it. The lines "to outlast brass," "our work shall pass," "than dew leaves upon grass," "no one will cry 'alas'," for example, have the same accent of a dying fall as Horace's "et fuga temporum" (1.5), "cum tacita virgine pontifex" (1.9), "ad Italos/Deduxisse modos" (11.13-14) and "cinge volens, Melpomene, comam." (1.16)[3]

The oracular strength of a poem such as "Body of John" derives from an employment of ironic contrast which is characteristic of Mason's very best work. While the grounding of the poem is not very far from his intuitive romanticism, the directly personal implications which invade much of his verse are not to be found here. A distancing, a kind of detachment, gives the poem its force. If it is the antithesis which makes it memorable, its balance of opposites could not have been achieved without this distancing. The poet compares his living lot with that of John, dead; but the terms of comparison inform us pointedly that there is little to choose between John's condition and that of the poet (or the poem's protagonist) himself. John's state is so described that *he* appears to be alive. As it happens, the whole poem is a comment on appearance and reality. That is one of its reverberations, but, if we may judge from Mason's other work, he had little sense of that theme.

If, in "Body of John" the irony lies in the close link between "the comfortable and the basic in life," in "Lullaby and Neck-Verse," another poem of similar construction, these two aspects of human existence are opposed (the tension between them is claimed, by Savage, to be the poet's "major theme."[4] "Lullaby and Neck-Verse" has power, but its success is limited because its details run counter to its antithetical construction. An extra element confuses the contrast. The condemned man is compared with his own protected childhood, his fate with the fate of Jesus. A further implication is thereby made possible, comparison of the condemned man's mother with Mary, but the basic theme is blurred by over-many implications and this is not helped by the weak line, "There is not any hope." Although it was not first published until the late nineteen-fifties, Curnow ascribes "Lullaby and Neck-Verse" to the 1924-30 period, thereby placing it as a product of the same impulse as "Body of John." Such a poem as "Tribute," again from that same period, shows one of Mason's primary strengths. Christ's visit to the "weak and poor" sinner is described in twelve short lines. In the scope of a brief lyric, Mason has reduced a dramatic situation adroitly to its basic elements. Carefully generalized as the poem is, the impressions gained from it are vivid.

No particular technical advance is evident in the poems of *Penny Broadsheet*. Where these poems, like most of Mason's work, are now always printed in the "hanging indent" form, in their originally published form this was not so. The more conventional lay-out was used. Some of the images, adjectives and "props" (skulls, etc.) show the influence of Beddoes, evident already in *In the Manner of Men*. Internal evidence suggests that "Oils and Ointments" may have been written as early as the earliest published poems (e.g., use of jewel images, hard objects).

A New Economy

Mason's most prolific period as a poet was in the late nineteen-twenties, and work in his fullest single collection, *No New Thing* (1934), had been done by the end of the decade. Range of technique, variety of line and stanza, is greater here than in earlier work. A new economy of means occasionally combines with the necessary detachment to produce such fine poems as "On the Swag" and "Judas Iscariot." Both poems serve to show also the considerable mastery he has acquired in using feminine endings and unstressed line-endings. Some of the latter poem's strength is gained from each line's starting with a strong beat or a monosyllabic word, thus being anchored to the page. Once this pattern is established an emotional crescendo, rooted in irony, is achieved. The rising tone is accomplished by "freeing" some of the lines, so that they begin "indeed," "that," and "and the," "all the," "and," "that," "oh," "that," "that," — with the emphases pushed forward to the centres or endings of the lines. Towards the end there are fewer feminine endings, and none at all in the final stanza.

The sustained flowing rhythm of "Nox Perpetua Dormienda" (*CP*, p. 69) which is used again later, with subtle variation, in "Flow at Full Moon" (*CP*, p. 94) is akin to Irish rhythms—those in the "traditional" Irish ballads of the eighteenth and nineteenth centuries, of the "Come-all-ye" and of the "art" ballads and "art" songs of Thomas Moore and others. Comparable rhythmical qualities may be found in some of Yeats's early poetry. The ground-pattern of the lines, in these two Mason poems, is such that, usually, each line is composed of five units:

> Your spirit/flows out/over all/the land/between
> your spirit/flows out/as gentle/and limpid/as milk
> flows on/down ridge/ and through valley/as soft/and serene
> as the light/ of the moon/that sifts down/through its light/
> sieve of silk.

In "Nox Perpetua Dormienda":

> Your eyeballs/dark/like a deep/black pool/in the night
> that is lit/by the steadfast/fire/of a handful/of stars.

Both are examples of great prosodic subtlety, but I have measured the lines as "breathing units" or "cadence units," counting in syllables rather than feet.[5] They lend themselves to this kind

of analysis, each line containing five "breathing units." One
example from Yeats will serve to draw the parallel:

You waves/though you dance/by my feet/like children/at play,
Though you glow/and you glance/though you purr/and you dart;
In the Junes/that were warmer/than these are/the waves/were
    more gay,
When I/was a boy/with never/a crack/in my heart.

The herring/are not/in the tides/as they were/ of old;
My sorrow!/for many/a creak/gave the creel/in the cart
That carried/the take/to Sligo/town/to be sold,
When I/was a boy/with never/a crack/in my heart.[6]

Part of Mason's technique in these and other poems is in
shrewd placing of words. He has an instinct for it, which enables
him to dispense with a great deal of formal punctuation. We
discover that the same poem, printed first in a newspaper or
magazine and later collected, is in nearly every case much more
heavily punctuated in the earlier version.[7] For one who uses
punctuation so sparingly, he employs the colon and dash to a
surprising extent. (He once said in conversation, "The reason
why I like the colon is because it looks so well on the page"!)

Early Loss of Urgency

The poems in *End of Day* do not sustain the powerful impression given by those in the larger book. "Prelude" (*CP*, p. 81)
and "Payment" (*CP*, p. 82) have the pared simplicity characteristic of Mason's best. As poems they do not "do" much.
"Prelude" merely suggests symbolically the use of "sword" in a
conventional way. "Payment" sounds portentous, but there is
little behind its statement that the poet has been subject to
passion, now regrets it, and has no friend to help him through
the rough moments. Somehow, in spite of all we know of him
through his earlier poems, this one has no hinterland of association. "Fugue" (*CP*, p. 84) and "New Life" (*CP*, p. 85) also
illustrate some loss of personal force. With its "dead-polluted
shore," "charnel-clutches," "ghosts," etc. "Fugue" reminds us of
Beddoes. This was one of a relatively small number of poems

Mason wrote during the Great Depression, which affected him profoundly.

We have no evidence that the technical strength of his work resulted from a conscious fostering of his own talent. The technique of juxtaposition (based partly on line arrangement) which he employed in such poems as "Body of John," "Lullaby and Neck-Verse" and "Lugete O Veneres" may for a moment, not too fancifully, be likened to that Pound, Williams and Eliot were using during the same period. For them, obviously, the method had wide-ranging possibilities involving the whole of history and a wide range of cultures. Mason did nothing to develop the technique and may have happened on it by chance or taken it from a much lesser source. He is narrow in outlook and has had no conception of the cultural eclecticism of the American poets. Juxtaposition was, however, well suited to the dualism of life and death which was the fundamental tension in his psyche. In that ultimate condition lay his one telling antithesis.

For a poet whose work is coming more and more to be regarded as the fruit of a gift sent by the gods, of intuition, he managed the problem of punctuation extremely well. We may find in, say, Dylan Thomas's "Poem in October" an example of beautiful, flowing force which has been gained as the poet fought free of punctuation. This is a virtuosity Mason cannot match, but we have everywhere in his work evidence that he can cut clean away from conventional punctuation and shape poems without relying on it at all. Had he been working in a local tradition and had there been an accumulation of penetrating local criticism, it is arguable that he might have gone much further, achieved a great deal more. Against such an argument must be put Stead's contention that Mason's was an intuitive talent which began to dissipate precisely at the moment it became self-conscious.

Mason's View of the Poet

Mason's life as a poet occurred almost wholly in the 'twenties and 'thirties. During the 'twenties his one important relationship was with Rex Fairburn and we have Mason's account of that, in the Auckland University valediction. From the evidence of the Fairburn letters quoted on that occasion there was between them some sort of dialogue on poetry, but we have so far no material representing Mason's part in it. Fairburn published a number of essays setting out his thoughts and ideas on New Zealand poetry, including one piece on Mason.[8] Mason himself apparently had little or nothing theoretical to contribute to the subject, although much later, in the late 'forties, he several times wrote and spoke on the subject of theatre. He seems not to have reacted to Fairburn's suggestions on poetry in any way—for example, the interesting plea made more than thirty years ago that we should look to the Americans, "our eldest brothers,"[9] rather than the English.

The first sharply intelligent critical force to arrive in our poetry was Allen Curnow, who began working in the very early 'thirties. As a critic, however, his real effect begins in the 'forties, once he had begun to realize fully the implications, for his own poetry and for New Zealand poetry as a whole, of being a New Zealander. He gave us, as we have seen, the earliest penetrating criticism of Mason's work. If we discount Fairburn's claiming an American connection, Curnow's is also the earliest criticism we have at the "philosophical" level and, whether or not one agrees with it, it is still the most incisive and influential at that level. Whether Mason could have benefited from it is another matter. As it happens, Curnow's work came too late for this to be possible. Instead Mason had to assess his own position and established his attitude to poetry entirely alone. This fact of itself endows his work, for us, with something of a heroic quality.

As poets the contrast between Mason and Curnow could hardly be more complete. Curnow has developed a poetry the strength and emotional impact of which depends on syntactical and intellectual compression. As he himself has observed, Mason's is a "natural" poetry, a kind which well exemplifies Keats's remark that "Poetry should come as naturally as the leaves to a tree." It is a "literature of the senses" or, to see from a different point of view, it deals directly with feelings, with no conscious attempt to distance them or project them. We may say that its excellence, or falling short of it, depends on *tone* or on the exact dramatic evaluation of moments in the "continual allegory" of his own existence.

If the tone is right or the evaluation exact, however, we feel that this is less due in Mason to hard-headed theory made over than to a simple sense of himself as poet. A feature of our poetry is that manifestoes have not often come from the poets. Reading in the letters of Yeats or Pound or William Carlos Williams some of us may regret the absence here of that cross-fertilization which is a product of mutual regard for each other's work. We carry the English distrust of groups and group theories to an extreme, so that, on the whole, we keep a "stiff upper lip" not only with regard to our own work but also that of others. This is one reason for the paucity of "philosophical" criticism here such as is offered in America by Allen Tate and others. For the same reason our criticism is largely in the destructive and too determinedly rational hands of the academics.

Mason has published few observations on his own practice and intentions, but something of these may be gleaned from the poetry itself. His earliest work exhibits a conception of the poem as subjectively dramatic, with the poet at the dramatic centre. This accounts for what may be described as the "Shakespearean" quality of "Sonnets at the Ocean's Base." His technical and conceptual range are shown more fully in *The Beggar*, where the obvious Classical influence suggests the possible gain of a degree of objectivity, which may however be merely the adoption of an attitude already, in itself, stylized and holding a personal appeal for him because of its implicit antithesis of life and death (see, for example, "The Lesser Stars"). The same antithesis is evident in the terms of "Song of Allegiance," with its revealing list of Romantic poets. The list itself, of course, tells us something of Mason's approach to poetry. In organization the poem offers further possibilities. Certain aspects of his procedure cannot be confirmed, or even properly discussed, until we have access to working drafts of the poems. "Song of Allegiance" may well be an example of one of the approaches to the poem put forward by Valéry and Eliot, where the tightly-organized form was the "given" element, the bones upon which Mason built for us a structure revealing his affinities and his sense of vocation. Apart from the absence of non-romantic poets from his list the requirements of the form may lead us to trust the poem as an instinctive gesture towards vocation and, to some extent, to distrust the roll call as arbitrary.

In some poems, Mason, by transference, apparently subscribes to the notion of "suffering poet." It is a chief token of his romanticism and it is probably by design that such a poem stands first in *No New Thing*:

> If the drink that satisfied
>   the son of Mary when he died
>   has not the right smack for you
>   leave it for a kindlier brew.
>
> For my bitter verses are
>   sponges steeped in vinegar
>   useless to the happy-eyed
>   but handy for the crucified.

This attitude, that the poems themselves are "handy" to help one though the world's suffering, is echoed and amplified later in the same group of poems, where the same archetypal moment is used:

>   he was passed
> by even the worst of men at least sour wine.

His approach to poetry and the poet in "Flattering Unction" is puzzling. In itself this Shakespearean sonnet is far from being one of his better pieces. Two quatrains, the second and third, on the theme of "my eternal fame" are apparently a conventional gesture towards Shakespearean, or perhaps we should say traditional, attitudes to the poet's role. If we see Mason simply as a naive, intuitive poet there are many points in his work where this kind of disappointment, which amounts to a double failure, of the imagination and of self-criticism, will be encountered. Happily, the whole question is not quite so uncomplicated. Working, as he did, in almost total isolation, it is possible that he made in such poems as "Flattering Unction" failures of a different sort.

Returning again to the possibility that he is, in a sense, an inverted optimist, one stunted in outlook by poor training for the arts in a utilitarian society, it is possible also to read into this and other poems a contrast which is, intuitively, ironical, but which fails because he is not fully conscious of the weight of values being opposed to each other. The gesture, "I shall be known to many a mighty nation," is either heedlessly silly or otherwise Mason was, though perhaps not overtly, aware of the bombast of it as an answer to "flesh that's alive and raving/to smell and touch these girls. . . ." One can only observe such possibilities and not hope to resolve them. A little more self-awareness, on the one hand, or a more responsive environment, on the other might have saved him at every stage from some of the excesses of minor romantic poets. The seeds of irony are so often present that it is tempting to find they have taken root. As it is, the admixture here of depressive realities and popular attitudes may remind us of Barry Humphries saying that life in New Zealand is like a play by Strindberg, with music by Mantovani.

That possibility of irony is even more present in "Twenty Sixth October" (*CP*, pp. 92-93), which is the nearest Mason comes to a "philosophical" poem. The distinction he draws here between appearance and reality is nowhere else made explicit in his poetry. More faithfully dealt with, the poem's central situation is not unlike that of "Flattering Unction." The same separation between art and life is implied, but now they are seen to separate and merge, to overlap and interchange. The whole performance is quite germane to Mason's view of the poet's role. It comes near to James K. Baxter's conception, in *The Fire and the Anvil* some years later, of the artist as performing a "ritual act."[10] Artist and "man alone" are identified, and the "ritual act" itself is conceived in terms, of a night journey:

> down a dull road I trudged
> hunched by a sky drawn close and smudged . . .
> far down a dreary road must travel

and old man shuffling weary gravel
in night and pain timorous alone

Taken as a whole, this is a curious poem, incoherent and
wide-ranging, with a degree of "thinking" in it which is extraordinary for Mason. Again, we have to take care to realize that
much may be found in the poem which is far beyond his conscious intentions for it. The protagonist begins by assuming a
mask not rightfully his, apparently, wishing to seem as if he
will break into the "fortress" or "prison" to his love:

I strode with dry ironic gesture
posing a high byronic posture
towards your barred home

This "heroic" action is set against a sky which is an appropriately "well-lit cyclorama." When he arrives on the scene of
action, however, "in one pulse the actor died." At this level
the poem concerns the attempted bravado of a young man dis-
appointed in love. As such, it has a firm opening and maintains
strength and focus for fourteen lines or so before veering off
into hysteria. As a poem of frustrated love it disintegrates after
running one-third of its course. From other points of view, it
finds much greater depth when the poet loses control, even
though some of the detail is banal. That it is night in the poem
sets a limit to the range of consciousness of the "old man" or
magus into whom the failed Byron is transformed. Now his
poet's (or "actor's") role is perceived as his only protection in
the "unequal task" of living in, participating in, a mortal world:

Give back the grease-paint and the mask
for shield against my unequal task.

But before this prayer we have had the contrast of "ironic
gesture" with a spontaneous overflow of powerful feelings, so
powerful it were as if, from the firmament so impressively posed
before us,

> the great Cross glittered at the pole
> Orion and his wrath were red
> and the Milky Way white overhead,

"one wild star," the protagonist's wildly disrupted life, "nor keeps the course of its appointment."

Besides being a conventional picture of the shattering effect of love denied, the poem appears to choose in its process between conscious art and possession. The image of the "wild star" apart, that section of the poem which becomes urgent in "lamentation" also loses point and compression, so that the execrable placement of the *vers trouvé* "the ulcer burst beneath the ointment" throws the whole piece out of key. Untidy as it is, "Twenty Sixth October" may still make us question Stead's conclusion that Mason was an intuitive poet whose impulse became vitiated at the point when he began to be conscious of himself in the role. The present poem may equally well be read as the beginning of a new phase, one which, had the poet been able to work through it, would have produced accomplished poetry of a different kind, in which the "ironic gesture" was not only wished for but realized.

Poet as Chronicler

The note at the end of *No New Thing* speaking of "a sort of Odyssey expressing the whole history of New Zealand" suggests that, by 1934 at the latest (since the note itself could have been written near the date of the book's publication), Mason had arrived at some sense of the poet beyond the romantically subjective, as recorder of his external world. The reference to Homer may, on the other hand, simply suggest that he had in mind the ancient idea of poetry as a record and celebration of great deeds.

By the time he wrote the "Prelude" for *This Dark Will Lighten* (1941, or a little earlier) he saw the poet as rejector of outworn tradition, of the misshaping influence of history, and as prophet of the "new," which is described in terms of dancing and feasting (and is thereby connected to his "dance drama" *China,* of the same period). His poems, he says, have been infected by the "desolation of the past," but this is no longer of importance. Whatever hint we may find in "Twenty-Sixth October" of a new phase of poetry in which intuition is interpenetrated with thought, is soon lost at this point. At the very juncture where he might well have pared away subjectively free-playing attitudes and tried to fix on the "thing in itself" as the proper object of poetry we discover him moving along a wrong track on which he has never retraced his steps. Allied with this move is a view of drama which would not today be widely accepted. His ultimate conception of the poet's role is apparently that stated in the prefatory remarks of *China* and applied in the late "Sonnet to MacArthur's Eyes" (*CP*, p. 103):

If our poets studied dramatic needs, then not only would that art perhaps benefit, but also it might act as a cross-fertilizing agent on poetry: which—despite Verlaine and even possibly at the cost of a slight rash of 'O Liberty's'—could profit with a little rhetoric with its resulting comprehensibility.

From the time of *China* onwards Mason has been preoccupied mainly with political and union journalism and, to a lesser extent, with drama. For whatever reasons, his most productive period as a poet had come to an end when he was in his middle thirties.

CHAPTER TWELVE

Conclusion

FROM being regarded simply as a Puritanical pessimist whose career was foreshortened when his attention was diverted to political activity, Mason has come to seem a much more complex person, and one in whom the apparent contradictions are not easy to reconcile. It is a paradox that he first chose, or was driven, to make real poems and began doing so at one of the grimmest points in the country's history only to stop when both the political and the publishing situations had greatly improved. He seems to have recognized his vocation when the oppressive Massey regime had still two years in office ahead of it, and to have virtually abandoned that vocation at a time when New Zealand's strongest Labour Government was flourishing.

It was Allen Curnow who first penetrated to the hard core of real value in Mason's work. Because of his own preoccupations, Curnow deplored the pioneers' lack of true contact with their adopted land and then went on to show that the attitudes of their immediate descendants were even less real because they had not even seen the "Home" which figured so largely in their thoughts and disfigured all their attempted imaginative flights.

For a long time, especially in the circumstances in which later writers were striving not to be oppressed by it, Curnow's apparent chauvinism seemed to be responsible for an exaggeration, even a distortion of view, when he insisted on "the distinctively native-born character" of Mason's poetry. The more Mason's work is read and the more it is related to the social background of the 'twenties and 'thirties and the work of other writers of the time, such as Sargeson and John Mulgan, the closer to the mark Curnow now seems to be. It is, perhaps, going too far to suggest, as he does, that Mason's work affords us "some glimpse into the unconscious mind of this island community," but it is to the point. Whatever attitude we may choose to see in such a poem as "Sonnet of Brotherhood," whether or not we seek overt or superficial signs of national identification in Mason's poetry as a whole, we cannot fail to recognize that it carries compressed in its gaunt texture the *feeling* of New Zealand in the 'twenties and 'thirties. The melancholy, puritanism and narrowness commonly read into his work by his own countrymen are, as much as anything, his instinctive response to the communal life.

When Professor J.C. Reid remarks that Mason's work expresses "the dominant spirit of the New Zealand secular intellectual," he does not go deep enough. The "dominant spirit" of New Zealand, intellectual and otherwise, *is* secular. Mason's poetry is probably the least secular we have in that he is always concerned with the problem of mortality and the desire to prolong one's individual self. Much of his work is directly Christian in its reference. Neither does he seem, finally, to be a typical intellectual. His attitudes—left-wing, liberal and quasi-pacifist— are in themselves pervasive among New Zealand intellectuals; but beyond that his approach to problems, his attempts to solve them, are usually intuitive rather than intellectual or even logical.

To describe his attitudes as quasi-pacifist brings us to a paradox in his way of looking at life. It has been said that, apart from the obvious one through trading in primary produce, New Zealand's chief links with the outside world are through war and sport. The rugby field and the war memorial are likely to be the most prominent communal features in any New Zealand town or settlement. These suggest the largely Anglo-Saxon origins of the New Zealand *pakeha*, and the nationwide scattering of monuments in the form of statues, parks and community halls, erected to commemorate New Zealand's part in two World Wars, tell also of the country's close link with, and indeed dependence on, Britain—a tie which is only now, and now partly because of the exigencies of trade and defence, becoming less close.

Perhaps because of his pride in Celtic origins, Mason has never been particularly fond of the British race nor of its rulers. Against tyrannical rule, he is prepared to approve of aggression. One of his images of heroism is the Irish struggle against Britain through the nineteenth and early twentieth centuries, another is of the Maori warriors fighting in the "iniquitous" Wars waged upon them by the British garrisons in the eighteen-sixties and 'seventies. More than one of his friends saw him as revolutionary in spirit. Rex Fairburn's poem "Lines for a Rebel" was originally written for him and, in the 'thirties, when he was most excited by the struggle and progress of the Chinese revolutionary armies, Mason himself could exhort:

> Get your machine-guns manned
> for a new way of war.

As against all this he shows, in his short pre-1939 play, "To save democracy," for example, or in the MacArthur sonnet, a typical liberalist tendency to be against war as such.

When Roger Savage is inclined to dismiss Mason's work as "so many versified notes for an autobiography" he shows, as might be expected, his limited experience of New Zealand poetry at that point. Of all our poets only Curnow and Smithyman have consistently attempted to work on a different plane from the autobiographical. Smithyman has even remarked, with a rare suggestion of irritation, on what he sees as our poets' all-pervading gambit of treating poems as if they are short stories of a particular kind. Mason in this respect is not exceptional, though it is true that many of his "versified notes" are not distanced from him in the manner some of our later poets have used to treat the personal lyric.

At their best, however, his poems are well above Savage's charge. Again it was Curnow who first discerned the element of joy in Mason's poetry, not in the direct statement but in the momentum of the verse. This possibility, that the work is more than the musings of a mere pessimist, has been commonly overlooked and is yet, as we have seen, present in Mason's very earliest poems, in, for example, that upsurge at the conclusion of "Out from Sea-Bondage."

Somewhat later, in his poems written as a response to reading Catullus, the absolute divorce between the states of life and death comes to the thematic forefront. He lacks the sophistication and arrogance of the Roman poet, but the ultimate strength of a poem such as "Nox Perpetua Dormienda" is in its affirmation of life. Death is thoroughly a preoccupation of his work. Yet even the powerful, stabbing lines of "In Perpetuum Vale," shortening, hauling in the Tennysonian source from which it derives, to shape what is perhaps his barest statement of mortal despair, have at the back of them a lost sense of the "divinity" of flesh, driven out by death-knowledge, but there to begin with.

Although he never systematically examines its implications, Mason often voices a conviction that life itself is, as Tolstoi thought of war, governed by chance. Every cosmic fact, from our planet's being "fixed at the friendless outer edge of space," to the poet's hand being a fortuitous gathering of atoms, is accidental. Such a view would, unmodified, tend to rule out any possibility of his subscribing to a religious solution to life as he saw it. Yet it leads him, at a crucial point, in the "Miracle of Life" to celebrate the chance nature of human existence. We may suggest, then, that the central tension of his poetry is intuitive, and that he is not a systematic or even a consistent thinker.

It is no great distance from "shocked faith" to despairing disbelief. Throughout the poems a strong feeling of sensuality struggles with knowledge of inevitable death. Grief is always and everywhere for the decay of the body, the passing of earthly life. Even a sense of possible perfection will not suffice to alleviate knowledge of inevitable "earth-toll."

Particularly when he was writing the poems in *The Beggar*, Mason was intensely engaged in the problem of death and what expectation of it does to us, to our psyches. The adaptation of Horace's "O Fons Bandusiae" apart, all sixteen poems are thematically involved in mortality-immortality. While undeniably Mason's finest poems are a handful in *No New Thing*, *The Beggar* is his most coherent book. The title poem, which opens the collection, presents us with a double contrast—a life of relaxation and ease set against death in poverty. The protagonist cannot enjoy the pleasures of this life because he is continually confronted by others' pain and death. As if in sequence, this is followed by a statement of the "agnostic's" dilemma (the poem would be more exactly titled "The Amoralist"), who can discover nothing of the moral categories in this life, but who apparently realizes that distinctions must be made. Here one dimension of the poem does not really get beyond the title. Within it the protagonist is aware of his own amoralism, but only in the title is it suggested that this involves non-engagement with the idea of God and therefore, by extension, no faith in an after-life. The title apart, these implications are carried in "The Agnostic" in Mason's ironical use of language.

Further implications are explored when we progress to "After Death," where the book's first truly elegiac note is struck. More emotionally subjective than the first two poems, "After Death," is also more powerful. It reverberates in a way characteristic of Mason's finest work. Having conveyed earlier that he cannot enjoy the present because of his awareness of pain and death and that he cannot achieve any sense of a future life, the protagonist now laments mutability purely from his own point of view: that the pleasures and beauties of earth shall abide even though he passes away. These two poems combined, "The Agnostic" and "After Death," work in the same field of operations as Wallace Stevens's great "Sunday Morning" sequence, and while it would be ludicrous to suggest any likeness between Stevens's urbanity and "The Agnostic," "After Death" is much more worthy of the comparison. It is formally and organically right for the emotion which charges it.

"Old Memories of Earth" is linked with "The Agnostic," and may perhaps be a development from it. Beginning with a statement agnostic in its implications it goes on to repeat the realization of mortality, deplores the existence of organized religion, suggests that the protagonist has a strong sense of the past and concludes in stating a sense of spiritual presence now almost lost to him. This sense of lost spirituality leads naturally on to the stark waking nightmare of "The Vigil," in which is gathered up, the protagonist's intuition of the finality of his own death. One aspect of this, one of Mason's least-regarded poems, which is usually overlooked is the verbal and rhythmical presentation of the theme, "Never ask for whom the bell tolls, it tolls for thee." In terms of the progression of *The Beggar*, as a whole, it evokes again that sense of the spiritual, although here the betrayal of it, with an ambiguity which allows us to include the possibility of the protagonist's ultimate sense of his own spirituality.

As if in counterpoint, "The Lesser Stars" returns to considerations of annihilation and oblivion already attached to the agnosticism of preceding poems. Now it is the work itself which comes under scrutiny. Even through our earthly achievements we shall not be remembered, and the following "In Perpetuum Vale" adds yet another aspect to the tension in our lives between life and death. The suggestion in the opening stanza that the protagonist once thought his flesh "divine" has behind it an implied contrast or opposition between childhood innocence and the period after he "knowledge-cup had quaffed." This is to say that one of the necessary features of earthly maturity is recognition of inescapable death. Because of it, from one point of view the lot of the living and dead is ultimately the same and this is part of the irony of "Body of John," where those who are not dead are, in any case, "perishing" and aware of it. Yet against this, in spite of our bondage to death, life itself is always the miracle.

If what has been said so far is true, that *The Beggar* has unity of theme based on emotional unity, Curnow's claim for "Sonnet of Brotherhood" as a distinctly "New Zealand" poem is diminished. Or rather, the poet's consciousness of its possibilities is unlikely. Its emotional rightness as a New Zealand poem is undeniable, and it will no doubt continue to be cited as documentary evidence of the growth of our national sensibility. From that point of view, we are lucky to have it. In the scheme of things, however, insofar as *The Beggar* has a "scheme," it appears to be a stoical or existential document, one of the few moments in Mason's work where "brotherhood" is acknowledged at any emotional depth. What it also offers is a tenuous link with the Universal or the One. It is remarkable that, intention and conscious considerations apart, there is in so many of these poems a spiritual sense, a sense of the Eternal, but at a vast distance. Here it is that distance, combined with an overwhelming realization of the inevitability of human fate, which creates the working tension of the sonnet.

In the following poem, "Wayfarers," we can see Mason attempting to come to terms with another dimension, time. His relating of the local environment with his own Classical and literary preoccupations does carry a kind of conviction, but it is only a subjective one. We cannot claim that this sense of the past inheres in our land in any way. Mason himself does not here transmogrify them into anything other than themselves. Even for him they remain, in Allen Curnow's tactful phrase, "dual realities." The ironically titled "Tribute" to Jesus seems to offer a gesture of belief which culminates in a sense of futility and perhaps implies agnosticism, adding another facet to the presentation of protagonist as "lack-faith."

With the two sonnets, "The Spark's Farewell," we move back to the firsthand involvement in body's death. Here it is to wonder what, if anything, the human "spark" gains by living this life. Again there is that vague apprehension of other possibilities, of a more spiritual plane of development, but this is immediately lost, giving place to a feeling of deprivation at the recollection of physical death.

Then, as in "The Lesser Stars," "Herostratus at Ephesus" considers the value of survival through reputation. Mason's attitude to the subject is always ambiguous. He makes this gesture, towards claiming an immortal reputation even at the cost of life itself, more than once. Here, however, the context, the way in which Herostratus's act is regarded, suggests it is seen by him at the deepest level as an act of useless bravado, even though the actual statement seems to claim some kind of success for the Roman. Two lines from "Wayfarers," touching on the same incident, clearly show the ambivalence of Mason's response to it. In imagination at least, he has:

> Burnt Dian's temple down at Otahuhu
> and slain Herostratus at Papatoe.

Following this recognition of unity in *The Beggar*, it is interesting that "Latter-Day Geography Lesson" should bring the book to a virtual close on a note of tough humour. The value of this poem, and possibly the reason for its positioning, is partly in showing that Mason can distance himself even from his obsessive theme of death. If the Horace adaptation, the final poem, has no other place in the book's unity it extends this sense of the poet's objectivity. One cannot, at this stage anyway, know what his conscious intentions were concerning the arrangement of *The Beggar*, but, instinctively, or otherwise, in it he made a book thematically cohesive in which the modulations in tone from one poem to another are accounted for with discernment. Of all the sixteen poems none could have been a more appropriate conclusion that the two chosen. They put the remainder in a perspective which takes them beyond mere self-involvement.

If *No New Thing* is justly Mason's most famous single volume, it lacks the organic feeling of *The Beggar*. The death theme is carried over, to some extent made more literary through the influence of Housman. Other themes are added, or more fully realized, but the best poems of this volume are an advance on *The Beggar* through an enlivening of the technique, possibly by a more conscious control of it.

Looking at "On the Swag" and "Judas Iscariot" together, we are conscious, first, of a new authority of presentation. These poems are a high point of Mason's work, and are complementary. They contrast the solitary with the social figure, and it has been suggested above that they may be seen, from one view, as figures of the artist and anti-artist. Is Mason, also, to some extent, "of the devil's party without knowing it"? If "On the Swag" at some readings seems streaked with sentiment, "Judas Iscariot," its theme reinforced by the vital rhythms, may be read as a triumphant affirmation of *this* life over the promise of the next, an affirmation which Mason himself found so hard to achieve that he finally gave up the effort and settled for red dawns coming up from the East.

Lurking in the background of his poetry is the continuing possibility of belief in Christian faith. Here we must make a distinction. He himself has told us of his Christian training and this colours his earlier work. His sense of Christ throughout is, however, notably of Him as a human being. He nowhere links his own seeking to know the purpose of human existence with his continuing consciousness of the Christ-figure.

The so-called sexy aspect of his work is confined largely to *No New Thing* and there it may be read as an extension of the mortality-immortality theme into sexual experience both as the means of procreating life and of enjoying it most deeply. One of his finest poems, also one of his most profoundly sexual, is "Flow at Full Moon," which completes the whole cycle of his work from the "Sonnets of the Ocean's Base" and also seems to complete his treatment of the mortality-immortality theme by being a poem which, even organically, is an expression of emotional acceptance, near resignation.

In the poems grouped towards the end of *No New Thing* several suggest this resignation to death, although in none of these pieces is this attitude emotionally realized, as it is in "Flow at Full Moon." Possibly this more unruffled attitude to death derives from the reading of Housman, but it is followed by a curious turn. After such poems as "Wise at Last," a statement finally negative, we get "New Life" (the solitary new poem published in 1936) where the poet cries "I have stripped for the fight . . . I shall not strip again" published in *End of Day* alongside such aggressive gestures as "This short straight sword" ("Prelude") and "Youth at the Dance." "Youth at the Dance" does not ring true as a Mason poem. Like the "Prelude" especially written for *This Dark Will Lighten*, it has a feeling of externality.

As Mason's talent came to the surface, he also became more pessimistic in the true sense of the term. His later poems, apart from "Flow at Full Moon," are gestures repudiating earlier depths. What can we make of his increasingly political responses to the country which, in an intended grim joke, he named "Stalin's Cultural Siberia"? Compared with his best work, "Youth at the Dance" and even "Sonnet to MacArthur's Eyes" are superficial. The little poem called "Fugue" in *End of Day*, reveals a solipsism which his most earth-conscious early work denies simply by being. In some way difficult to locate precisely, this poem is evasive and literary. By the time he wrote it Mason appears to have succumbed to a state of extreme hopelessness from which he moved almost entirely into political journalism and non-poetry.

At the same time, he became more convinced of the possibility of making drama. All the plays on record are vitiated, first and foremost, by propagandist intent. This progressively deepening commitment to a poltical programme and a political faith can be seen as characteristic of New Zealand. It may, first, be a product of the country's conscious secularism, but far more is it the result of a materialist and utilitarian view of life. Spoken and unspoken, everywhere the attitude is held that every member of the community has a direct social responsibility to it. Artists are, as a rule, expected to make their work socially relevant, although the pressure to do so is unseen and is from the general communal climate rather than "the top."

Possibly, in becoming increasingly occupied with political matters, Mason has found his salvation as a man. If Stead's theory, that Mason was a "natural poet who lost his force with his spontaneity," is true, we may have lost little or nothing by the change. The uncomfortable conclusion we must reach, besides this one, is that in a richer cultural environment, Mason might well have made the transition, from being one kind of poet to being another, without accident.

A poet virtually wihout a tradition, it may well be asked what effect Mason's models, his chance reading and his education, had upon his work in general? Classical influence, his study and teaching of Catullus, Horace and others, was almost entirely beneficial. His temperament found an echoing mordancy, and his talent a proper astringency and economy, in those Roman poets. The effect of his English models—we should perhaps name Humbert Wolfe and Hardy with Beddoes, Housman and Tennyson—is much more problematic. Where he found kinship with both themes and tones in the Roman poets his responsive reading of Housman and the others appears to have been at a later, more self-conscious period. If news of Eliot and Pound reached New Zealand shores during the 'twenties, there is nothing to show for it unless we stretch rather a long way and see in, say, "Lullaby and Neck-Verse" a juxtaposing method not unlike that operated in "The Waste Land"!

At this late date, it may seem surprising that Harold Monro responded as he did to Mason's poems, particularly as Pound believed he had got Monro to begin to understand *his* ideas on poetry, which are of a different world; but Monro did, possibly recognizing in the work the "indestructible poet." Mason has always had his advocates among perceptive critics of poetry.

The Final Position

Finally, recognizing that he has added perhaps six or eight durable poems to our small stock, we may ask what else has R.A.K Mason contributed to our literature? Has he anything to offer poets of a later generation? He is usually named with Fairburn, Curnow and Glover as of the "thirties" poets. On the whole, the group has been over-discussed because of its unique position in New Zealand poetry, and to some extent over-valued for the same reason. It is usually said that, with them, New Zealand poetry truly began. They stand out in contrast to the situation at present, when something like twenty poets of good competence are active.

If these 'thirties poets have seemed to dominate the scene up to the immediate past, there remains very little valuable detailed criticism of their work, assessing their achievement and influence. Curnow's position must be secure, not only because of his widely acknowledged technical competence as a poet, but because of his creative contributions to the criticism of poetry. He has been prepared to make laws for himself and offer them to us. If later poets, by and large, have not so far matched his work in merit, the offerings of later critics are negative in comparison.

Mason's position is more equivocal. Of all our poets, he seems to have been least conscious of any relationship between criticism and poetry. His remarks on Verlaine in the preface to *China* are exceptional and, from any critical point of view outside his own work, ill-judged. The defects of his work are plain to see and have been sufficiently well indicated in Smithyman's pioneer critical work, *A Way of Saying*. Mason's romanticism is often only tenuously related to realities. Yet it remains true that he has given us, in "Judas Iscariot," "Footnote to John II, iv," "Flow at Full Moon," and perhaps half-a-dozen other poems, the most memorable contribution we have yet had from any of our poets.

It may be that later generations are too near his work for there to be any direct disciples among them. The kind of poetry we have at the moment, from our youngest "wave" of poets, exemplified perhaps in the toughness, lightness and wit of Brian Wigney's work, is a far remove from Mason's romanticism. Perhaps his work is of a kind we shall never come back to, and it is not, in that sense, usable. Whether this is so, or not, he has given us a number of poems we would not well be without again. For himself at least, his best work invalidates his own words opening "The Lesser Stars":

> We are they who are doomed to raise up no monuments
> to outlast brass:
> for even as quickly as our bodies' passing hence
> our work shall pass
> of us shall be no more memory left to any sense
> than dew leaves upon grass.

Appendix

MASON revised many poems for *No New Thing* and *This Dark Will Lighten*. Those in the "Poems from Mss. 1924-1930" section of *CP* were revised immediately prior to their inclusion in that volume.

1. With few exceptions, the revisions are of three kinds:

(a) removal of punctuation, except where it is necessary to the *sense* of the lines. "Song of Allegiance," for example, is conventionally punctuated in *Penny Broadsheet*, but in subsequent printings of the poem all punctuation is removed.

(b) from *No New Thing* onwards Mason habitually uses the hanging indent for forming his stanzas, with the first word of each stanza capitalized. Earlier poems and printings are usually organized so that indentation corresponds with rhyme. Poems in the earlier form were later modified to fit in with the general pattern adopted.

(c) a fair number of vocabulary changes are made from early to later versions of poems. Very often these changes are replacements of "poetic" language and word order by natural language and word order (e.g., from "The Lesser Stars"— "'tis" in *The Beggar* becomes "it's" in *This Dark Will Lighten*. "Times mind we . . ." in *The Beggar* becomes "At times we mind . . ." in *This Dark Will Lighten*).

2. "In Perpetuum Vale," as it is printed in *The Beggar*, has six stanzas. The last two of these are omitted in all subsequent printings of the poem, presumably on the grounds that they are less tightly organized than the remainder of the poem and, in any case, are thematically repetitive.

184

3. In *The Beggar*, "O Fons Bandusiae" has the note: "Spiritually rendered into English verse fairly closely after: 'Heigh-ho, My Fancy.'"

4. The version of "Flattering Unction" which appears in *The Auckland Sun* for Friday June 28, 1929, has a different ending from that of all book printings of the poem:

> Still, in the long run, they'll win and not I;
> They'll have the laugh when Eternity's gone by.

A weaker ending, this is interesting because it is more explicitly of a piece with Mason's characteristic balancing of sexual/physical fulfillment against the sense of mortality and longing for "eternal fame."

5. "Man and Beast" (*CP*, p. 75) was first printed in *The Auckland Sun* for Friday October 14, 1927. Typical revisions have been made, but the *Sun* version also included a third stanza subsequently omitted. Stanza 3 repeats the sense of stanza 2 and is bathetic in several important points of detail, hence its omission.

6. At least two other versions of "Their Sacrifice" (*CP*, p. 76) are in existence. A typescript copy of one of these was given to the present writer by the late A.R.D. Fairburn. This is dated August 7, 1930. Two lines of stanza 1 and the whole of stanza 3 differ substantially (in text, but not in sense) from the published version. Another version of the poem, used in the unpublished playscript *This Bird May Swing*, exists in typescript form in the possession of the author (and has been sighted by the present writer). This is closer to the "Fairburn" than to the published, version.

7. Perhaps a dozen of R.A.K. Mason's unpublished poems and epigrams are in circulation in typescript or manuscript. These presumably will remain unpublished as Mason himself has indicated the definitive nature of the *Collected Poems*.

Notes and References

The following abbreviations are used throughout the notes:

(B 31.) B with a numeral refers to an item listed in the selected bibliography. This method has been used because Sections 1 and 2 of the bibliography have the items listed in date order, while Section 3 is listed as the items occur in the text.

Penguin NZV = *The Penguin Book of New Zealand Verse.*
DI = *Discovered Isles* (B 21).
DLOW = *Distance Looks Our Way* (B 32).
PELHNZ = *The Pelican History of New Zealand.*
CP = R.A.K. Mason's *Collected Poems.*
On Fairburn = "R.A.K. Mason on Rex Fairburn."
Unamuno = *The Tragic Sense of Life* (B 43).

CHAPTER ONE

1. *Pakeha,* from the Maori, is the New Zealand name for a New Zealander of European ancestry.
2. Sir Charles Christopher Bowen (1830-1917), New Zealand's Minister of Justice in the mid-eighteen-seventies, published *Poems* (his only volume of verse) in 1861. These lines are from "The Old Year and the New," *Penguin NZV*, pp. 91-92 (B 25).
3. *Penguin NZV*, pp. 92-94.
4. Edward Tregear (1846-1931), was Secretary of Labour in the eighteen-nineties. He published *"Shadows" and Other Verses* in 1919. *Penguin NZV*, 95-96.
5. Keith Sinclair's biography of Reeves, a former Prime Minister of New Zealand, was published by Oxford University Press in 1965. Allen Curnow describes Reeves's own book *The Long White Cloud* (1898) as "still the best written account of New Zealand history." *Penguin NZV*, pp. 98-101.
6. *DL,* p. 17 (B 21).
7. *DLOW* (B 32).
8. *DLOW,* p. 44.
9. *DLOW,* p. 81.

10. *PELHNZ* (B 33). The whole of Part Three is relevant as a polished and succinct history of New Zealand from the outbreak of the First World War to the mid nineteen-fifties.
11. *PELHNZ*, p. 238.
12. *CP* (B 14).
13. *A Book of New Zealand Verse*, 1945 edn., p. 24 (B 22).
14. Lowell's essay "Edgar Allan Poe" (1845) is included in Edmund Wilson's *The Shock of Recognition* (New York, 1943), pp. 5-6.

CHAPTER TWO

1. On Fairburn, p. 16 (B 12).
2. *Ibid.*, p. 15.
3. Dr. A.W.H. West, now a member of the Department of Romance Languages, University of Auckland.
4. *AGS Chronicle*, the school magazine of Auckland Grammar School.
5. On Fairburn, p. 2.
6. Letter to present writer, 14 July, 1956.
7. *The Chapbook*, no. 39 (London, 1924), p. 29.
8. A.R.D. Fairburn, "A New Zealand poet." *New Zealand Artists' Annual*, 1929, p. 69.
9. On Fairburn, p. 10.
10. *Ibid.*, p. 4.
11. *Ibid.*, pp. 15-16.
12. *CP* introduction, p. 12.
13. *Ibid.*, p. 13.
14. J.E. Traue, *A Preliminary Checklist of Works by and about R.A.K. Mason* (B 29).
15. *Book*, no. 2, p. 18. The same issue includes Allen Curnow's early essay on Mason (B 19).
16. Sid Scott, *Rebel in a Wrong Cause*, pp. 138-139 (B 34).
17. Letter to present writer, 14 July, 1956.
18. "Mr. Kerridge tries culture." *Landfall*, no. 5, March 1948, pp. 34-38.
19. On 29 November 1950 it appeared in the *World Federation of Trade Unions Information Bulletin*, no. 46.
20. Traue, *Checklist*, p. 18.
21. On Fairburn, p. 2.
22. *China Dances* (Dunedin: printed by John McIndoe Ltd., 1962), p. 3 (B 15).

CHAPTER THREE

1. *CP* intro., p. 9.
2. *An Anthology of New Zealand Verse*, edited by Robert Chapman and Jonathan Bennett (London: Oxford University Press, 1956), preface, p. xxiii.
3. E. H. McCormick, *New Zealand Literature: A Survey* (London: Oxford University Press, 1959), pp. 111-120.
4. *Penguin NZV*, pp. 42-47.
5. *Book*, no. 2, pp. 3-7.
6. *Recent Poetry in New Zealand*, chosen and with an introduction by Charles Doyle (London and Auckland: Collins, 1965), p. 48.
7. *DI, The Deepening Stream*, p. 21.
8. *CP*, p. 31.
9. E. H. McCormick, *Letters and Art in New Zealand* (Wellington: New Zealand Department of Internal Affairs, 1940), p. 188.
10. Plomer, *Penguin New Writing*, no. 17, p. 151 (B 20).
11. *DI, The Waiting Hills*, p. 157.
12. *A Book of New Zealand Verse*, 1945 edn., intro. p. 32.
13. *Ibid.*, p. 26.
14. Alan Mulgan, *Literature and Authorship in New Zealand* (London: Allen and Unwin, Ltd., P.E.N. Books, 1943), p. 28.
15. *DI, The Deepening Stream*, p. 72.
16. J. C. Reid, *Creative Writing in New Zealand: a Brief Critical History*. Printed for the author by Whitcombe and Tombs Ltd., Auckland, 1946.
17. James K. Baxter, *The Fire and the Anvil: Notes on Modern Poetry* (Wellington: New Zealand University Press, 1955), pp. 72-73.
18. E. H. McCormick, *New Zealand Literature: A Survey* (London: Oxford, 1959); see especially pp. 114-117.
19. *CP* intro., p. 11.
20. Kendrick Smithyman, *A Way of Saying*, A Study of New Zealand Poetry (London and Auckland: Collins, 1965), p. 65.
21. *Landfall*, no. 67 (September 1963), pp. 286-290.
22. C. K. Stead, "R.A.K. Mason's Poetry—some random observations," *Comment*, no. 16 (July 1963), pp. 34-39.
23. C. K. Stead, "For the Hulk of the World's Between," *DLOW*, pp. 79-96.
24. *Comment*, no. 16, p. 34.

CHAPTER FOUR

1. Throughout this chapter I am indebted to Mr G. Hemus's unpublished paper, "Classical Feeling in the Poetry of R.A.K. Mason." This paper was presented at Auckland University in 1964 as one of the requirements for an M.A. (Honours) degree.
2. Hemus, p. 7.
3. Hemus, p. 8.
4. *Letters and Art in New Zealand*, p. 184.
5. *Richard III*, I, iv. *The Complete Works of William Shakespeare* (London: The Nonesuch Press, 1953), vol. II: Histories, p. 916.
6. *CP*, p. 22. In 1.7 "upleapt" is misprinted as "unleapt." In all earlier versions the reading is "upleapt."
7. W. H. Auden, *The Enchafèd Flood* (London: Faber, 1951), p. 19.
8. William James, *The Varieties of Religious Experience* (London: Longmans, Green and Co., 1904), pp. 142-143.
9. My rendering.
10. Some of my conclusions differ from those of Mr. Hemus. In the form in which they are expressed here all the conclusions are my responsibility.
11. Lionel Trilling, *The Liberal Imagination* (New York: The Viking Press, 1951), p. 199.
12. *Catullus—The Complete Poetry*, translated by Frank O. Copley (Ann Arbor: University of Michigan Press, 1957), pp. 3-4.
13. *Ibid.*, p. 6.
14. *The Collected Works of Horace*, translated by Lord Dunsany and Michael Oakley (London: Dent, Everyman's Library, 1961), p. 32.
15. *Ibid.*, p. 36.
16. *Ibid.*, p. 89.
17. This parallel is drawn by Hemus, but in somewhat different terms.
18. Dunsany and Oakley, p. 65.

CHAPTER FIVE

1. Spinoza, *Ethics*, edited with an intro. by George Santayana (London: Dent, Everyman's Library, 1910), p. 92.

2. Miguel de Unamuno, *The Tragic Sense of Life*, translated from the Spanish with an intro. by Amalia Elguera (London: Collins, Fontana Library, 1962), pp. 52-53.
3. Wallace Stevens, *Opus Posthumous* (New York: Knopf, 1957), "Adagia," p. 162.
4. *Comment*, no. 16, p. 36.
5. Roman Catholic doctrine, for example, holds that the blessed continue in the future life "with the same bodies and souls that they had," *Catechism*, Q and A 129.
6. Unamuno, p. 67.

CHAPTER SIX

1. *Penguin NZV*, p. 44.
2. "We'd both been brought up—both Rex and I had been brought up—in strict Anglican and Conservative traditions. They were good for us, too." (On Fairburn, p. 16.)
3. *Comment*, no. 16, p. 36.
4. In New Zealand, the term "man alone" probably originates with John Mulgan's novel of that name (1939), but the figure was a conscious one earlier than that.
5. *Penguin NZV*, p. 46.
6. In conversation with the present writer.
7. *Penguin NZV*, pp. 45-46.
8. In "Twenty-Sixth October," for example.
9. *Landfall*, no. 66 (June 1963), p. 190.
10. Paul Valéry, *The Art of Poetry, The Collected Works of Paul Valéry*, edited by Jackson Mathews, Vol. VII, translated by Denise Folliot, with an introduction by T. S. Eliot (London: Routledge and Kegan Paul, 1958), "Poetry and Abstract Thought," pp. 52-81.
11. The poem's background is the Arian heresy, Arius's denial of the con-substantiality of God the Father and God the Son. The Son existed before Time but is not immortal, although, Arius claims, all things are created by Him through the Father. James Joyce has a vivid paragraph on this in *Ulysses* (London: Bodley Head, 1937), p. 35: "Is that then the divine substance wherein Father and Son are con-substantial? Where is poor dear Arius to try conclusions? Warring his life long on the contransmagnificandjewbangtantiality. Ill-starred heresiarch. In a Greek water-closet he breathed his last: euthanasia."
12. Unamuno, p. 100.

CHAPTER SEVEN

1. *Opus Posthumous,* "Adagia," p. 176.
2. *No New Thing,* p. 68.
3. *Penguin NZV,* p. 43.
4. *Book,* no. 2.
5. *The Fire and the Anvil,* p. 71f.
6. *Penguin NZV,* p. 44.
7. The phrase is from Keith Sinclair's poem "Waitara," II, from *Strangers or Beasts* (Christchurch: The Caxton Press, 1954), p. 11. More than once, in his poetry, Professor Sinclair, a distinguished historian, gives us in a phrase a key imaginative insight into the New Zealander's situation and New Zealand's historical perspective.
8. *Strangers or Beasts,* pp. 11-12.
9. Alistair Campbell, *Mine Eyes Dazzle* (Christchurch: The Pegasus Press, 3rd ed., 1956), pp. 22-23.
10. More commonly than is usually supposed, Baxter and Mason share themes, attitudes, tones of voice. "Footnote to John, II, iv" may be compared with "The Homecoming" (from Baxter's *In Fires of No Return,* London, 1958, p. 33), or "Flow at Full Moon" with "Let Time Be Still" (*In Fires of No Return,* p. 12).
11. Rainer Marie Rilke, *The Notebooks of Malte Laurids Brigge* (New York: Capricorn, 1958), p. 145.

CHAPTER EIGHT

1. At least in terms of "book" publication. We know that the version of "O Fons Bandusiae," for one, was made some years earlier .
2. Note also the sexual implications of "Prelude" from *End of Day* (*CP,* p. 81):

> This short straight sword
> I got in Rome
> when Gaul's new lord
> came tramping home:
>
> It did that grim
> old rake to a T—
> if it did him,
> well, it does me.

> Leave the thing of pearls
> with silken tassels
> to priests and girls
> and currish vassals:
>
> Here's no fine cluster
> on the hilt, this drab
> blade lacks lustre—
> but it can stab.

3. Unamuno, pp. 35-36.
4. A.R.D. Fairburn, *Collected Poems* (Christchurch: The Pegasus Press, 1966), p. 220.

CHAPTER NINE

1. *CP* intro., p. 12.
2. *CP* intro., p. 13.
3. *Comment* no. 16, p. 39.
4. *New Zealand Literature: A Survey*, p. 116.
5. *In Print*, December 1944, p. 27.
6. *China*, preface.
7. *Refugee*. Copy of typescript (original?) given to present writer by J. E. Traue. See Traue *Checklist*.
8. *People's Voice*, December 21, 1943, p. 3.
9. *In Print* (March 1944), pp. 12-13.
10. Richard John Seddon (1845-1906), New Zealand prime minister, 1893-1906.

CHAPTER TEN

1. With the present writer, at Devonport, Auckland, in January, 1957.
2. Humbert Wolfe, *Out of Great Tribulation* (London: Gollancz, 1940), p. 18.
3. *A Way of Saying*, p. 80.
4. *Ibid.*, pp. 81-82.
5. *The Works of Thomas Lovell Beddoes*, edited with an introduction by H. W. Donner (London: Oxford University Press, 1935), p. 159. Book hereinafter referred to as *Beddoes*.
6. *CP* p. 60, p. 110, p. 62.
7. *Beddoes*, p. 112, "Doomsday."

8. *Ibid.,* p. 95
9. *Ibid.,* p. 115.
10. *Ibid.,* p. 93.
11. *Ibid.,* p. 11, lines 38-40.
12. *Ibid.,* p. 8, lines 103-106.
13. *CP* p. 27, p. 30, p. 21.
14. *Beddoes,* p. 103, lines 49-60.
15. *Ibid.,* p. 41, lines 39-42.
16. *CP* p. 22, p. 49, p. 38.
17. *Beddoes,* p. 74, lines 22-33.
18. *Ibid.,* p. 86. "Another letter to the same, from Goettingen; March, 1826," lines 1-4.
19. *Ibid.,* pp. 101-102.
20. *Ibid.,* p. 87, lines 53-70. Of incidental interest is Beddoes' use here of the colon, characteristic also of Mason.
21. *Beddoes,* p. 81. "Pygmalion," lines 157-168.
22. *Beddoes,* p. 155. "Stanzas Written in Switzerland" (fragment).
23. *Ibid.,* p. 90. "Resurrection Song."
24. *Ibid.,* p. 248. "Dream of Dying," lines 1-7.
25. *Ibid.,* pp. 56-57.
26. *Ibid.,* pp. 56-57.
27. *Outidana, or Effusions, Amorous, Pathetic and Fantastical. Beddoes,* pp. 59f. (Poems composed 1821-25.)
28. *Ibid.,* p. 75.
29. *Collected Poems,* London: Cape (1939), pp. 42-43.
30. *Ibid.,* p. 11.
31. *Ibid.,* p. 14.
32. *Ibid.,* p. 15.
33. *Ibid.,* p. 24.
34. *Ibid.,* p. 25.
35. Mason, *CP* p. 77 (my italic)
36. *A Shropshire Lad,* p. 58.

CHAPTER ELEVEN

1. *Comment,* no. 16, p. 35.
2. See note *CP,* p. 77, *No New Thing,* p. 28.
3. Hemus, 10-11.
4. *Landfall* no. 67, p. 290.
5. The kind of syllabic count used here is similar to that used by William Carlos Williams, Charles Olson and others (see, for example, Williams's 1954 letter to Richard Eberhart).

6. W. B. Yeats, *Collected Poems* (London: MacMillan, 2nd ed., 1950), p. 23, "The Meditation of the Old Fisherman." See also pp. 46, 62, 65, 69, 74—"The White Birds," "The Lover Tells of the Rose in His Heart," etc., characteristic rhythms of the early Yeats.

7. See Appendix on Revisions and Variant Readings.

8. See bibliography (B 18).

9. A.R.D. Fairburn, "Some Aspects of N.Z. Art and Letters," pp. 213-218.

10. *The Fire and the Anvil*, pp. 71-73.

Selected Bibliography

A. Primary Sources: Items by R.A.K. Mason
(chronologically arranged)

1. *In the Manner of Men.* Auckland: the author, 1923. Manuscript, in two copies.
2. *The Beggar.* Auckland: published by the author, 1924. Whitcombe and Tombs Ltd., printers.
3. *Penny Broadsheet.* Auckland: published by the author, 1925.
4. *No New Thing. Poems* 1924-1929. Auckland: The Spearhead Publishers, 1934.
5. *End of Day.* Christchurch: Caxton Press, 1936.
6. *Squire Speaks.* Christchurch: Caxton Press, 1938.
7. "To Save Democracy," a play. *Tomorrow,* 4(13), April 27, 1938, 408-411.
8. *Recent Poems* (With Allen Curnow, A.R.D. Fairburn and Denis Glover). Christchurch: Caxton Press, 1941.
9. *This Dark Will Lighten. Selected Poems,* 1923-1941. Christchurch: Caxton Press, 1941.
10. *China.* Script for a dance-drama by Margaret Barr. Auckland: printed by the Times Printing Works, 1943.
11. *Frontier Forsaken.* An Outline History of the Cook Islands. A "Challenge" Publication. Auckland: Johnston Press, printers, 1947.
12. "R.A.K. Mason on Rex Fairburn." A talk given to the Auckland University College Literary Society in April, 1957. Tape-recorded. Uncorrected typescript copy made 5 August, 1964.
13. "Writers in New Zealand: a questionnaire." *Landfall* 14 (1), March 1960, 58-60.
14. *Collected Poems.* With an Introduction by Allen Curnow. Christchurch: Pegasus Press, 1962.
15. *China Dances.* The original script for Margaret Barr's dance-drama (see Item 10 above), with other verses. Dunedin: John McIndoe Ltd., printer, 1962.
16. *Rex Fairburn by R.A.K. Mason 1962.* Dunedin: University of Otago English Department, 1962.

B. *Secondary Sources.*

(listed chronologically)

17. Donnelly, Ian. "Of N.Z. poets. Some notes and comments. No. 3. Mr. R.A.K. Mason." *Auckland Sun,* 21 December, 1928, p. 14; *Christchurch Sun,* 11 January, 1929, p. 6. Traue comments: "Quotes Harold Monro on Mason, probably from personal correspondence."
18. Fairburn, A.R.D. "A New Zealand poet." *New Zealand Artists' Annual,* 1929, p. 69.
19. Curnow, Allen. "The poetry of R.A.K. Mason." *Book* 2, (May, 1941), 3-7.
20. Plomer, William. "Some books from New Zealand." *Folios of New Writing* 4, Autumn 1941, 55-61. (Reprinted in *Penguin New Writing* 17, April-June, 1943, 149-154.)
21. Holcroft, M. H. *The Waiting Hills.* Wellington: Progressive Publishing Society, 1943, 72-74. (Reprinted in *Discovered Isles: a Trilogy,* Christchurch: Caxton Press, 1950, 162-164).
22. Curnow, Allen. *A Book of New Zealand Verse,* 1923-45. Christchurch: Caxton Press, 1945. Mason's work is discussed in the valuable Introduction, 26-33. (Revised to 1950, reprinted 1951. Mason discussed, Introduction, 24-30).
23. Reid, J. C. *Creative Writing in New Zealand; a Brief Critical History.* Printed for the author by Whitcombe and Tombs, Auckland, 1946. (Mason, 32-34.)
24. McCormick, E. H. *New Zealand Literature: a Survey.* London: Oxford University Press, 1959. (Mason, 114-117.)
25. Curnow, Allen. *The Penguin Book of New Zealand Verse,* Harmondsworth: Penguin, 1960. (Mason, Introduction, 42-46; Notes, 324-325.)
26. Broughton, W.S. "Sponges steeped in vinegar; a note on the *Collected Poems* of R.A.K. Mason." *Education* 12, 6 (July 1963), 16-18.
27. Savage, Roger. Review of Mason's *Collected Poems. Landfall* 67 (September 1963), 286-290.
28. Stead, C.K. "R.A.K. Mason's poetry—some random observations." *Comment* 16 (July 1963), 34-39.
29. Traue, J.E. *A Preliminary Checklist of Works by and about R.A.K. Mason.* Duplicated, revised to December, 1963.
30. Hemus, G.A. "Classical Feeling in the Poetry of R.A.K. Mason." Unpublished paper, University of Auckland, 1964.
31. Smithyman, Kendrick. *A Way of Saying.* London and Auckland: Collins, 1965. (Mason, 64-67 and throughout.)

32. *Distance Looks Our Way:* The Effects of Remoteness on New Zealand, ed. by Keith Sinclair. Auckland: published by Paul's Book Arcade for the University of Auckland, 1961.
33. Sinclair, Keith. *A History of New Zealand.* London: Pelican Books, 1959.
34. Scott, Sid. *Rebel in a Wrong Cause.* Auckland and London: Collins, 1960.
35. *Recent Poetry in New Zealand,* chosen and with an introduction by Charles Doyle. Auckland and London: Collins, 1965.
36. Mulgan, Alan. *Literature and Authorship in New Zealand.* London: Allen and Unwin Ltd., P.E.N. Books, 1943.
37. Baxter, James K. *The Fire and the Anvil,* Notes on Modern Poetry. Wellington: New Zealand University Press, 1955.
38. Auden, W.H. *The Enchafèd Flood.* London: Faber, 1951.
39. James, William. *The Varieties of Religious Experience.* London: Longmans, Green, 1904.
40. *Catullus—The Complete Poetry,* translated by Frank O. Copley. Ann Arbor: University of Michigan Press, 1957.
41. *The Collected Works of Horace,* translated by Lord Dunsany and Michael Oakley. London: Dent, Everyman's Library, 1961.
42. Unamuno, Miguel de. *The Tragic Sense of Life,* translated from the Spanish, with an introduction by Amalia Elguera. London: Collins, Fontana Library, 1962.
43. Mulgan, John. *Man Alone.* London: Selwyn and Blount, 1939. (Latest reprint, Paul's Book Arcade, Hamilton, New Zealand, 1965).
44. Valéry, Paul. *The Art of Poetry.* The Collected Works of Paul Valéry ed. by Jackson Mathews, Vol. VII, translated by Denise Folliot, with an introduction by T.S. Eliot. London: Routledge and Kegan Paul, 1958.
45. Wolfe, Humbert. *Out of Great Tribulation.* London: Gollancz, 1940.
46. *The Works of Thomas Lovell Beddoes,* ed. with an introduction by H. W. Donner. London: Oxford, 1935.
47. Housman, A.E. *Collected Poems* London: Cape, 1939.

Index